Artist Eugene J. Martin's Secret Hieroglyphs

Suzanne Fredericq

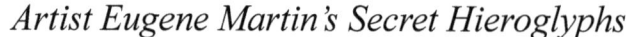
ISBN: 978-0-9825704-5-6

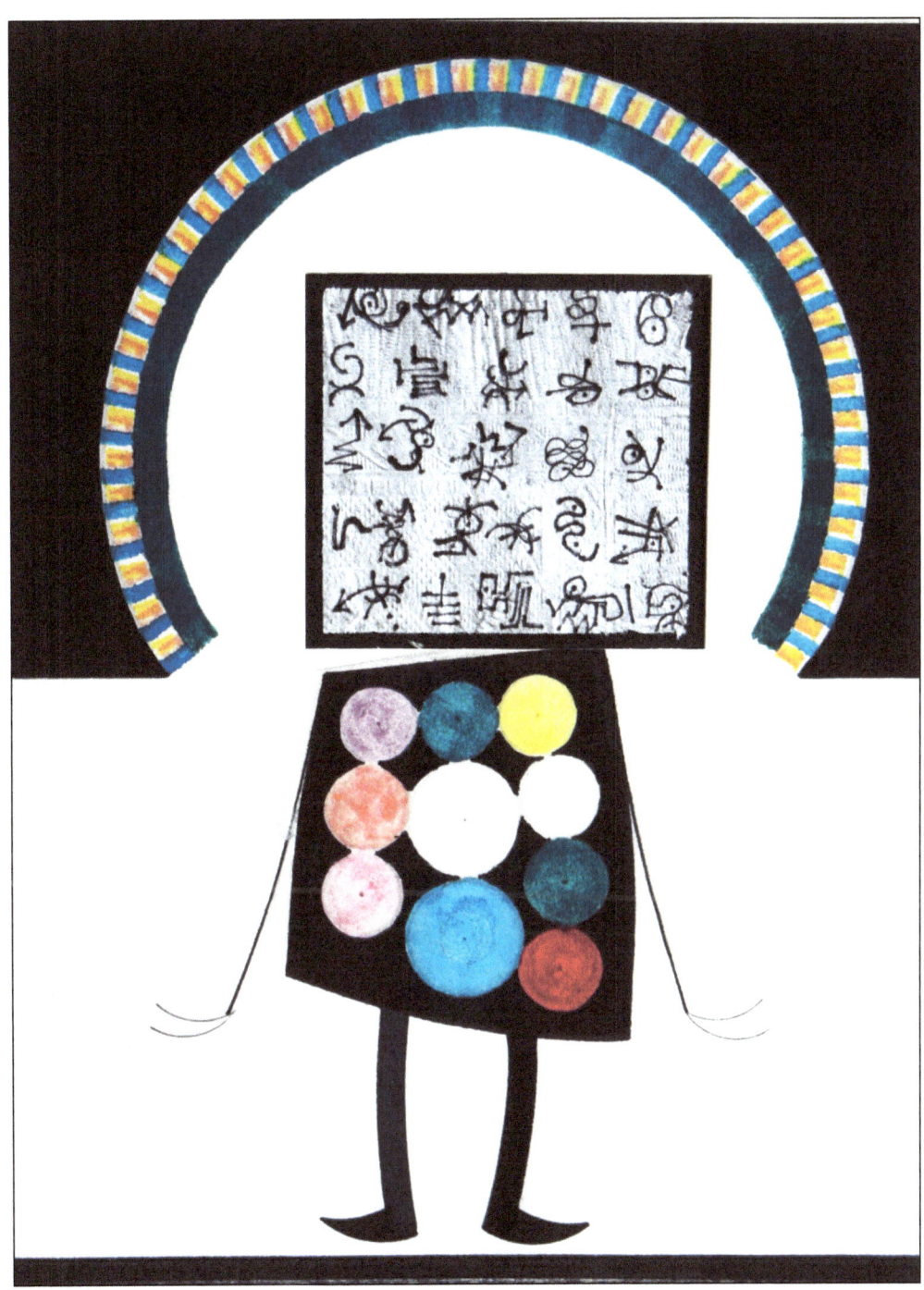

Pen & ink on paper napkin incorporated in untitled mixed media work on paper, s.d. (1970's), 9.5x6 3/4"

Foreword

When Eugene Martin couldn't afford drawing paper in the mid-1970', he would make pen and ink drawings on paper napkins. A hieroglyphic archetype would suddenly appear. He would later incorporate many of these napkin drawings in mixed media collages in the late 1980's and 1990's in Washington D.C. and Lafayette LA. Other secret languages were written down with graphite pencil and pen & ink on regular paper.

Suzanne Fredericq,
Lafayette, Louisiana, November 3, 2009

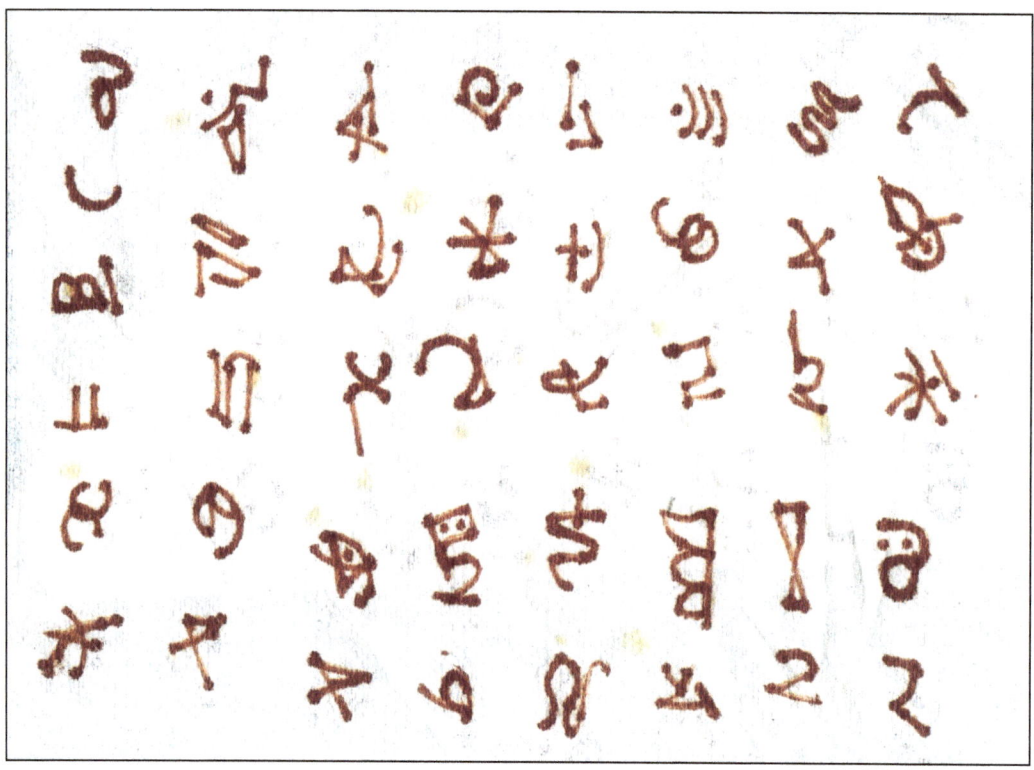

Untitled pen and ink on folded napkin, s.d., 5x3.5"

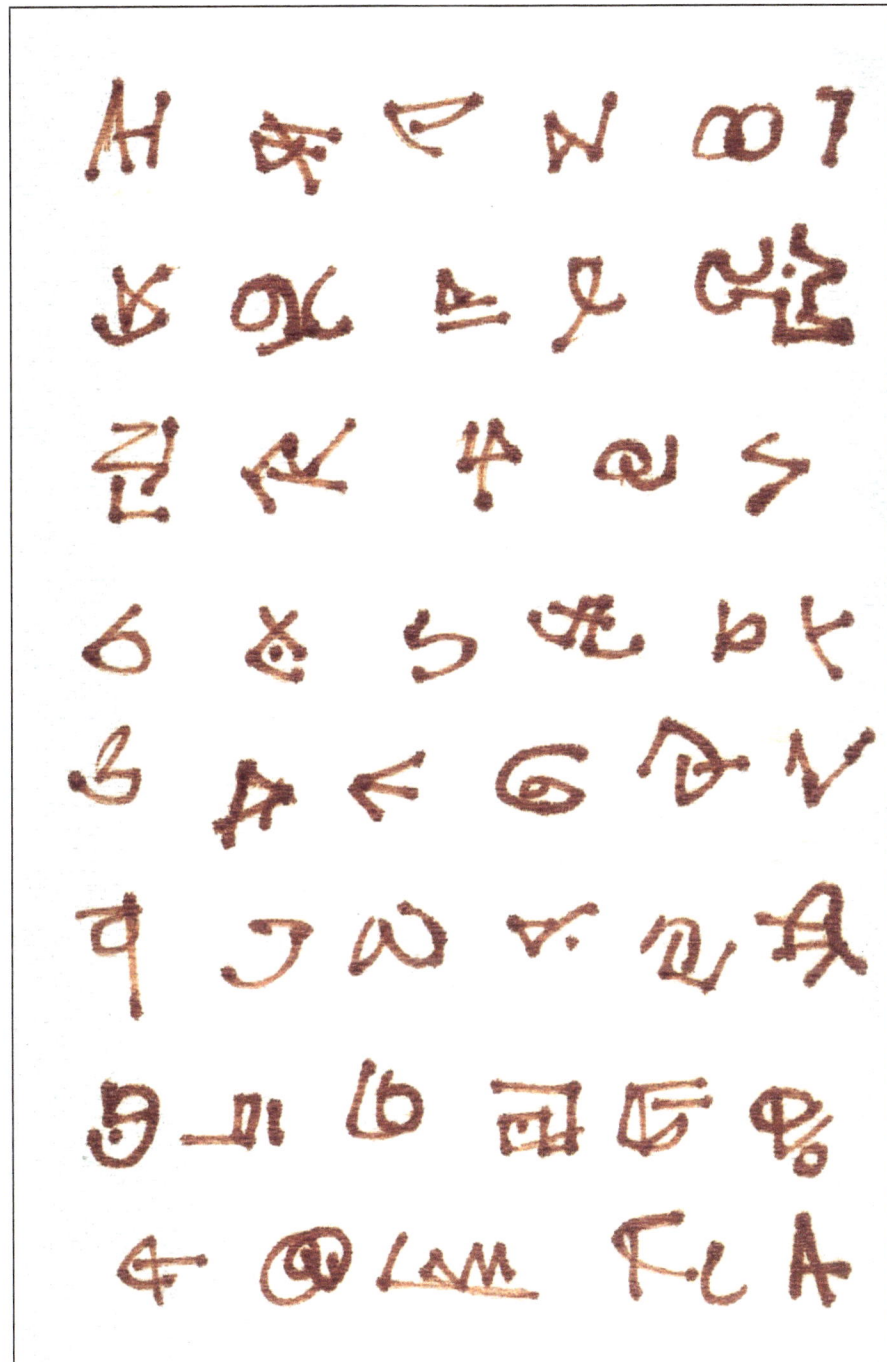

Untitled pen and ink on folded napkin, s.d., 5x3.5"

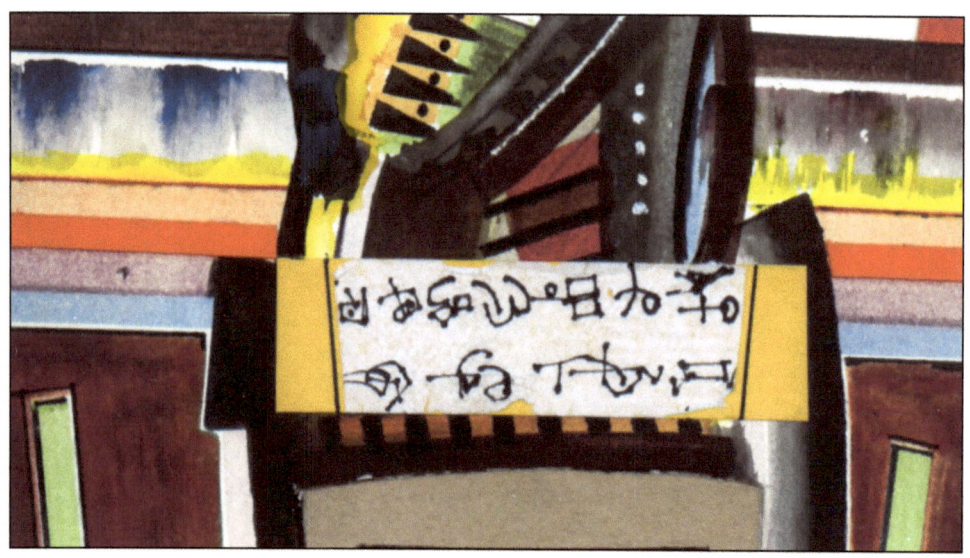

Untitled mixed media collage at right, and close-up above, s.d., 10x8"

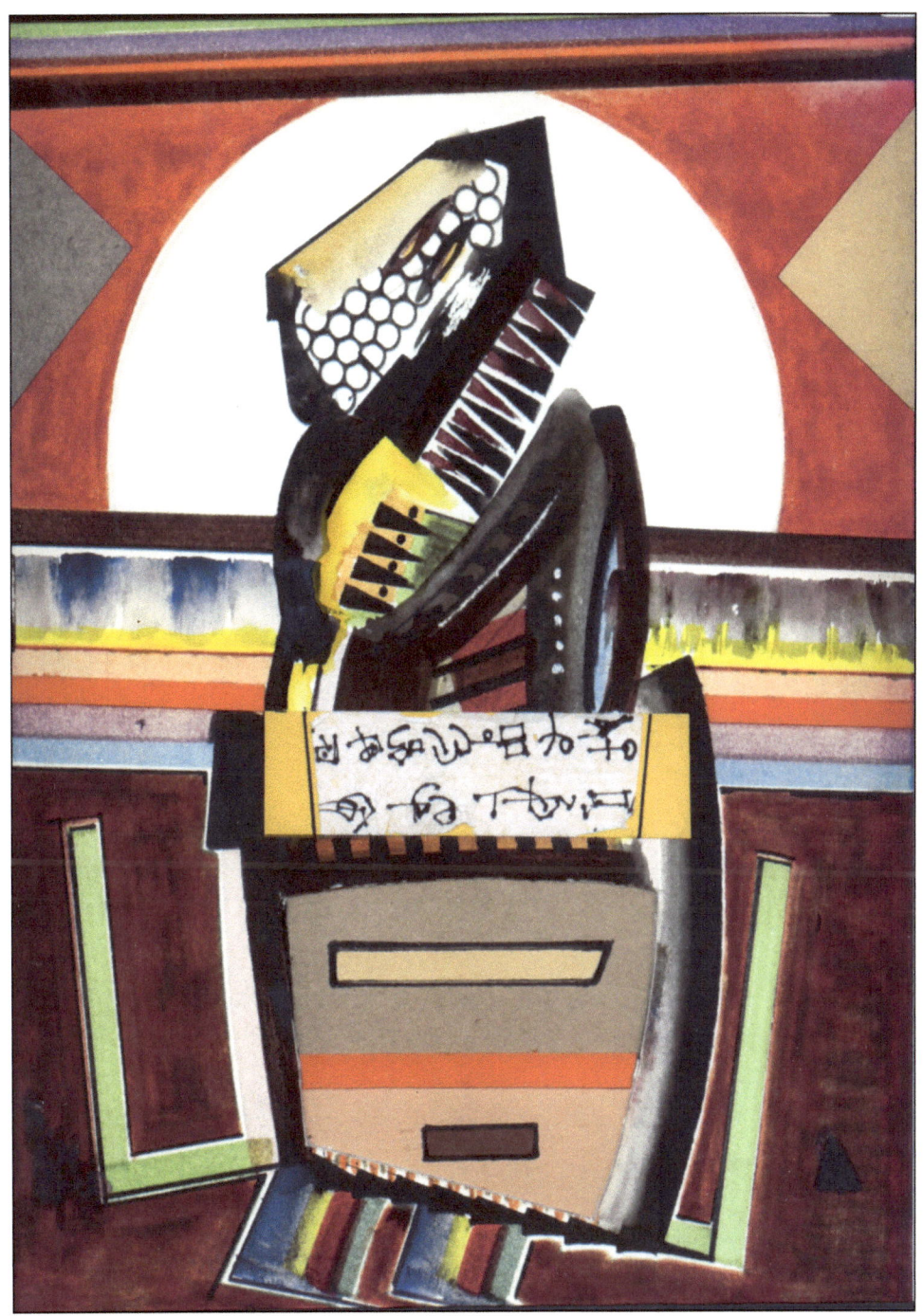

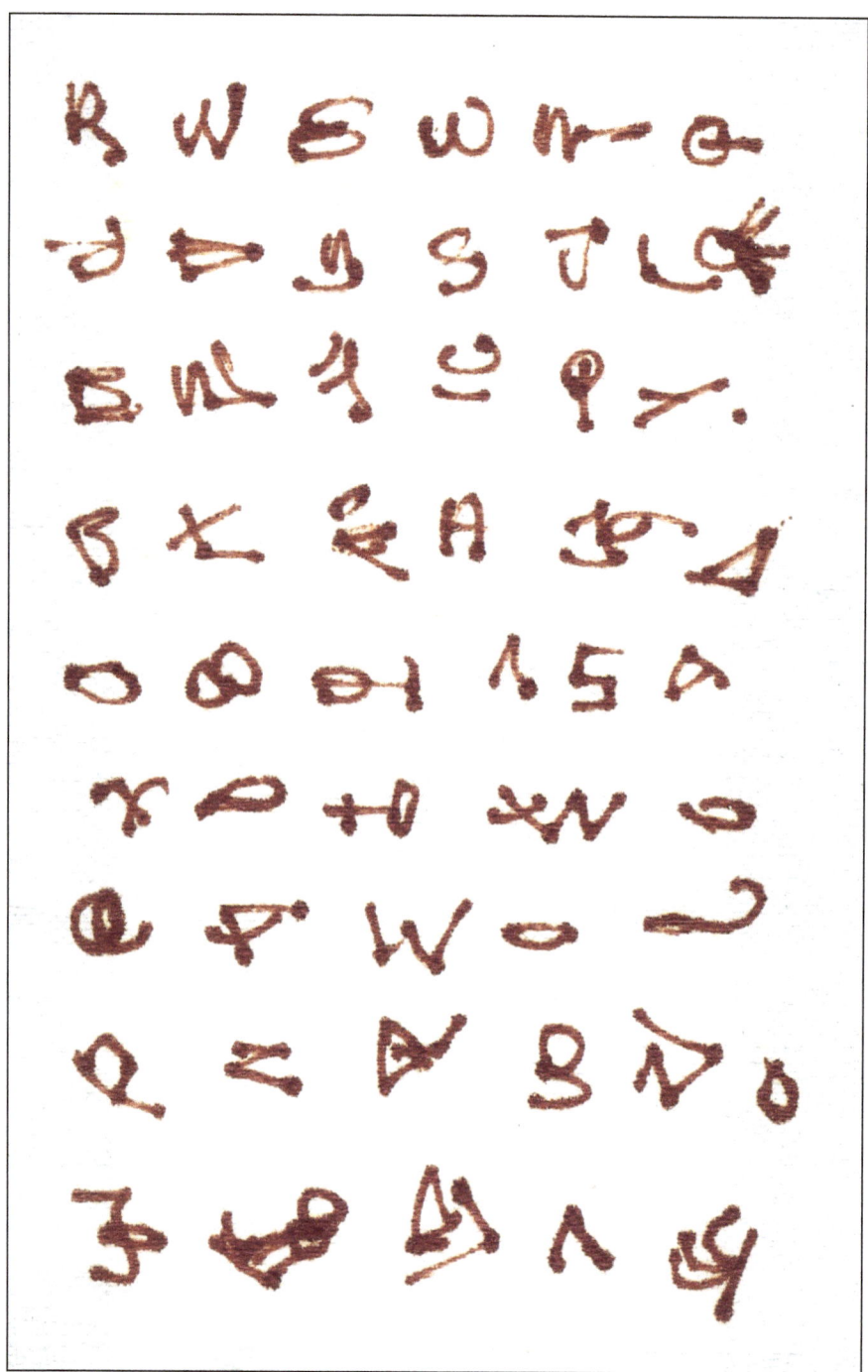

Untitled pen and ink on folded napkin, s.d., 5x3.5"

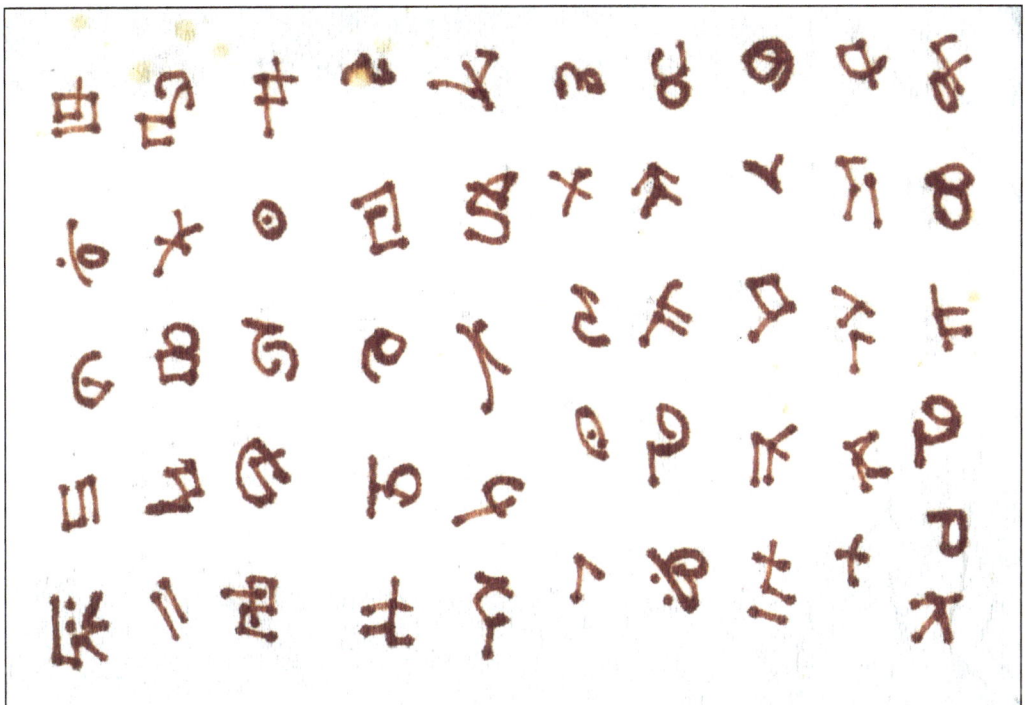

Untitled pen and ink on folded napkin, s.d., 5x3.5"

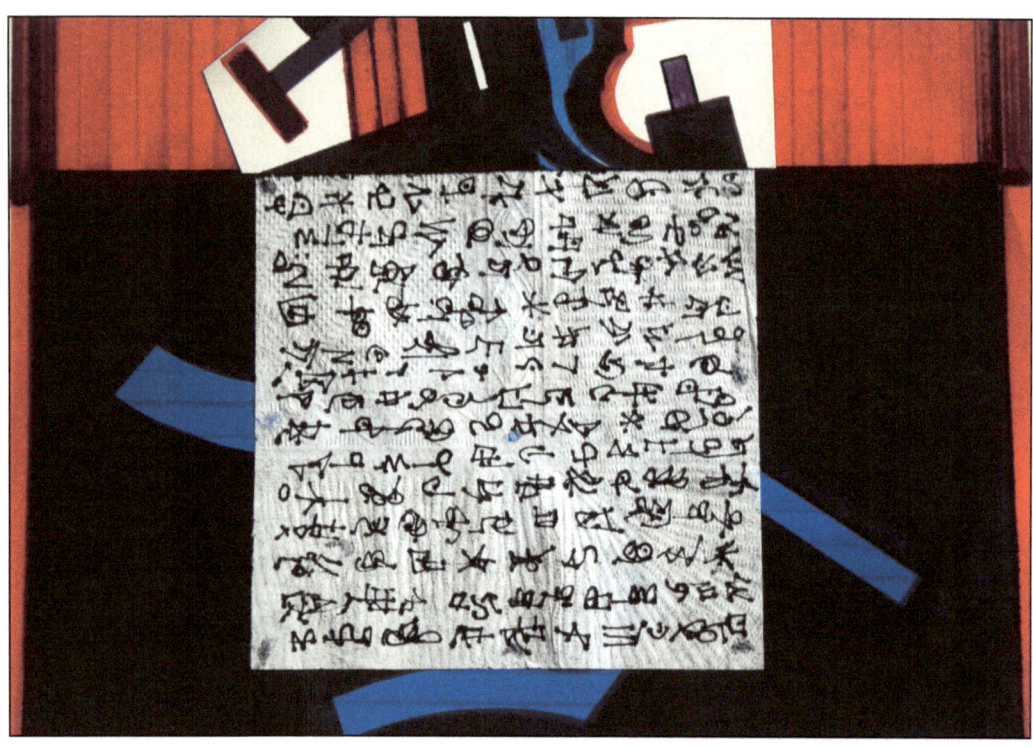

Untitled mixed media collage at right, and close-up above, s.d., 10x8"

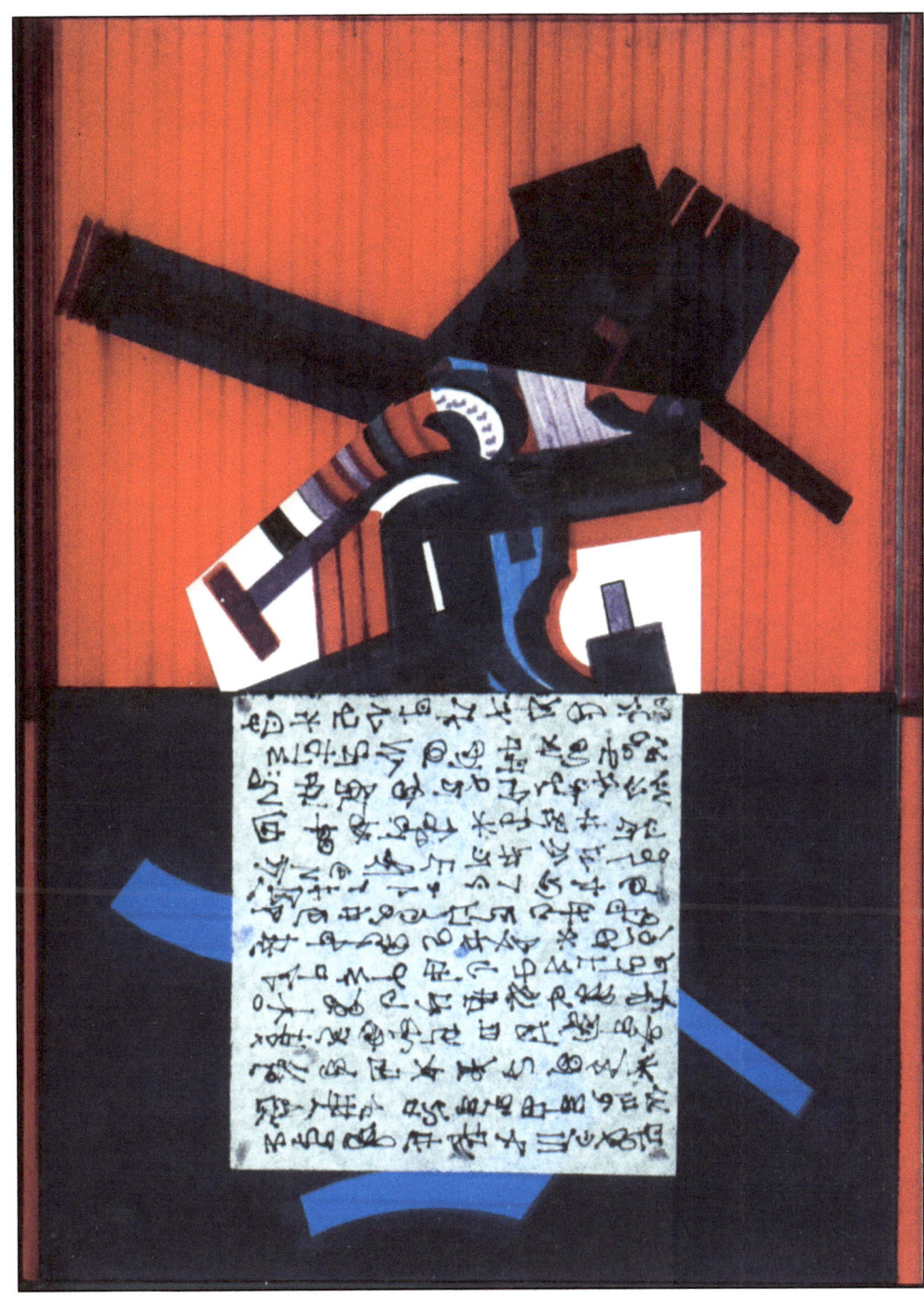

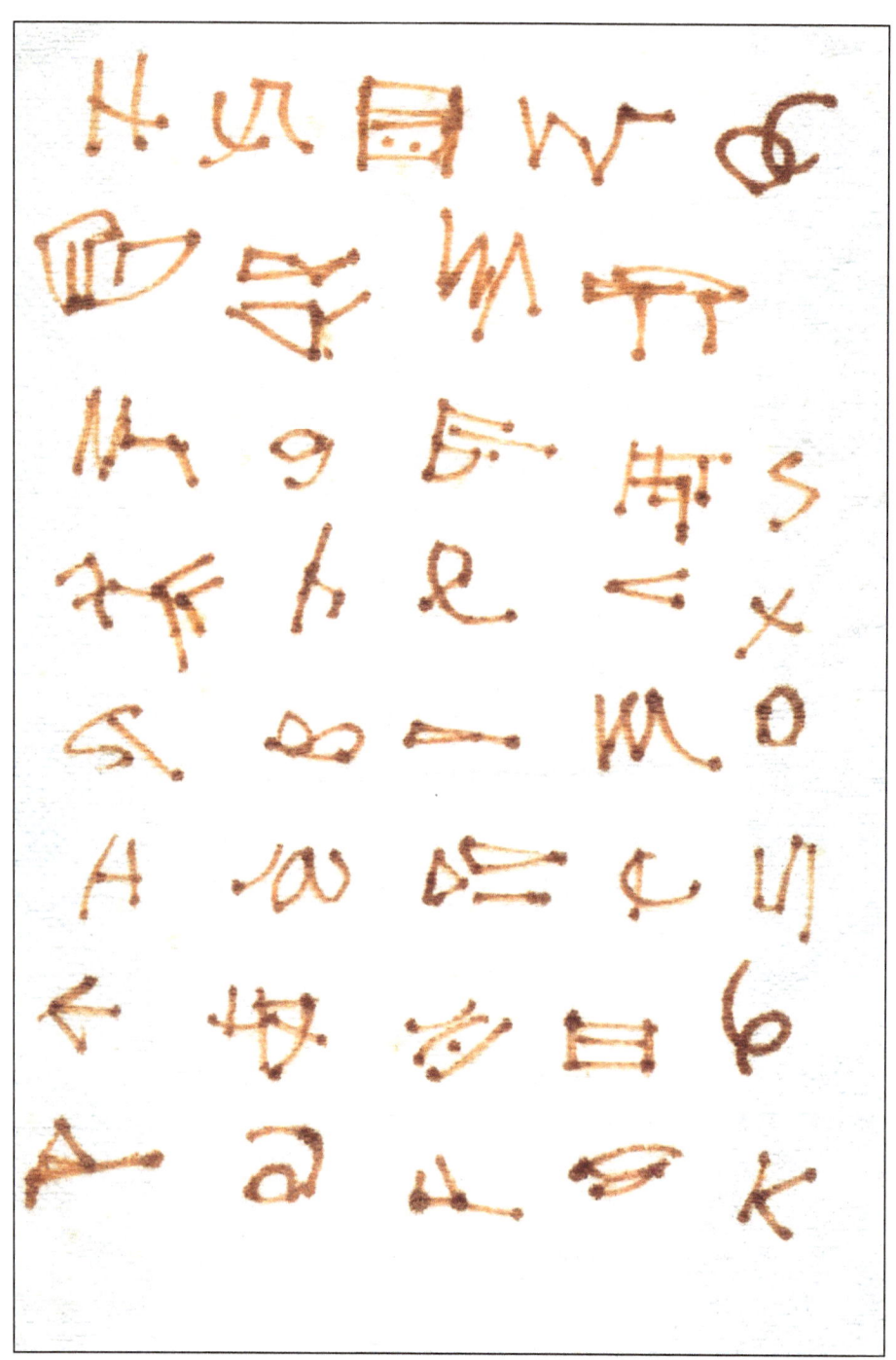

Untitled pen and ink on folded napkin, s.d., 5x3.5"

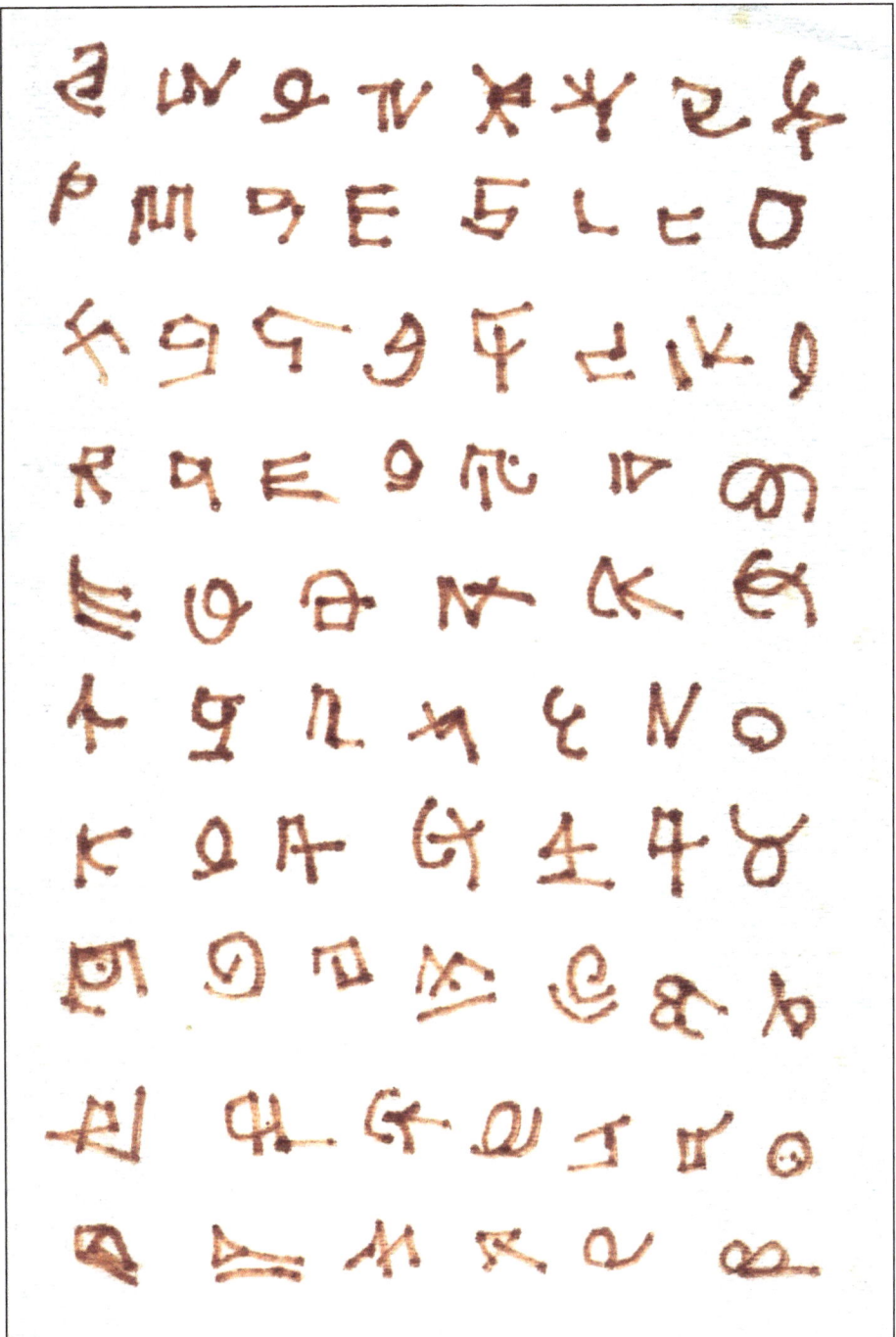

Untitled pen and ink on folded napkin, s.d., 5x3.5"

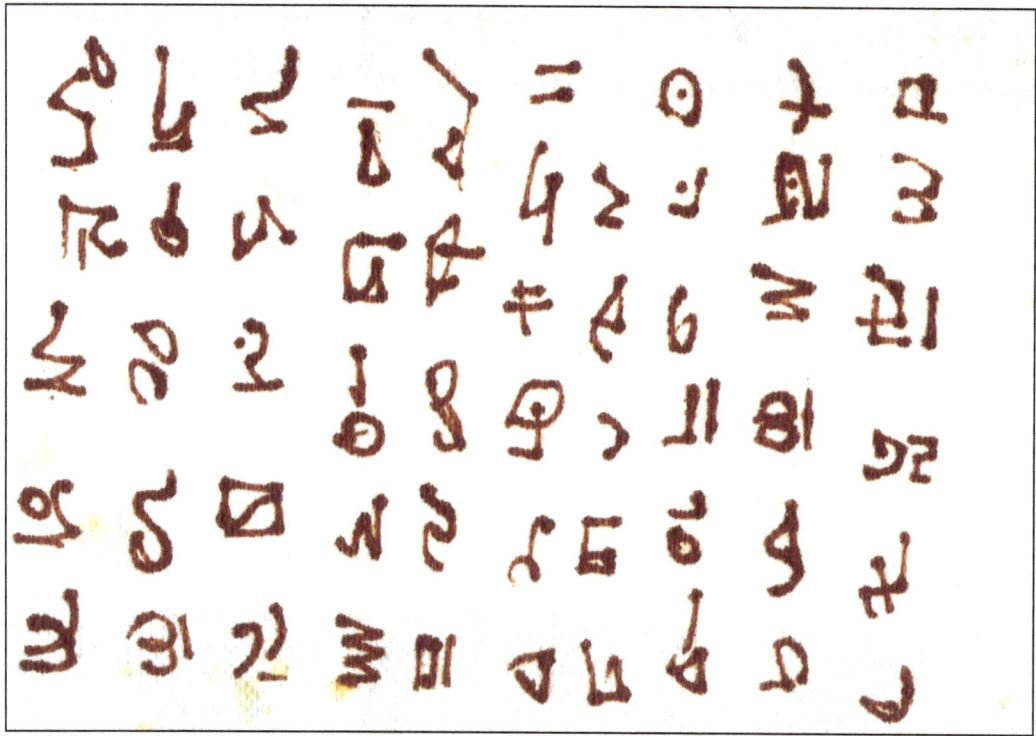

Untitled pen and ink on folded napkin, s.d., 5x3.5"

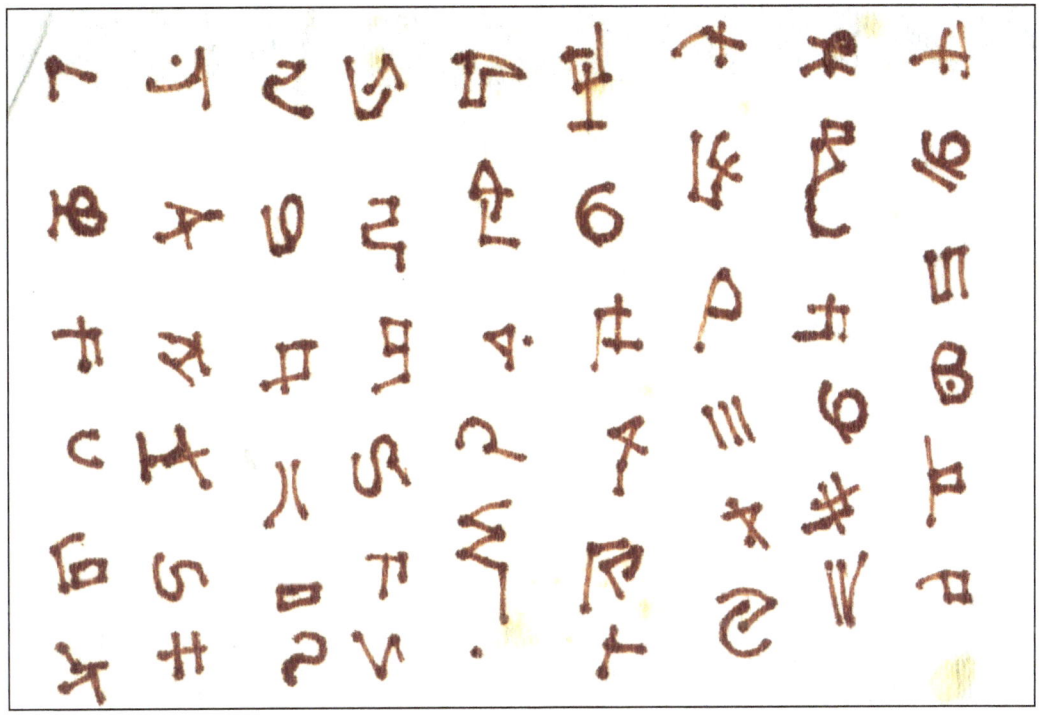

Untitled pen and ink on folded napkin, s.d., 5x3.5"

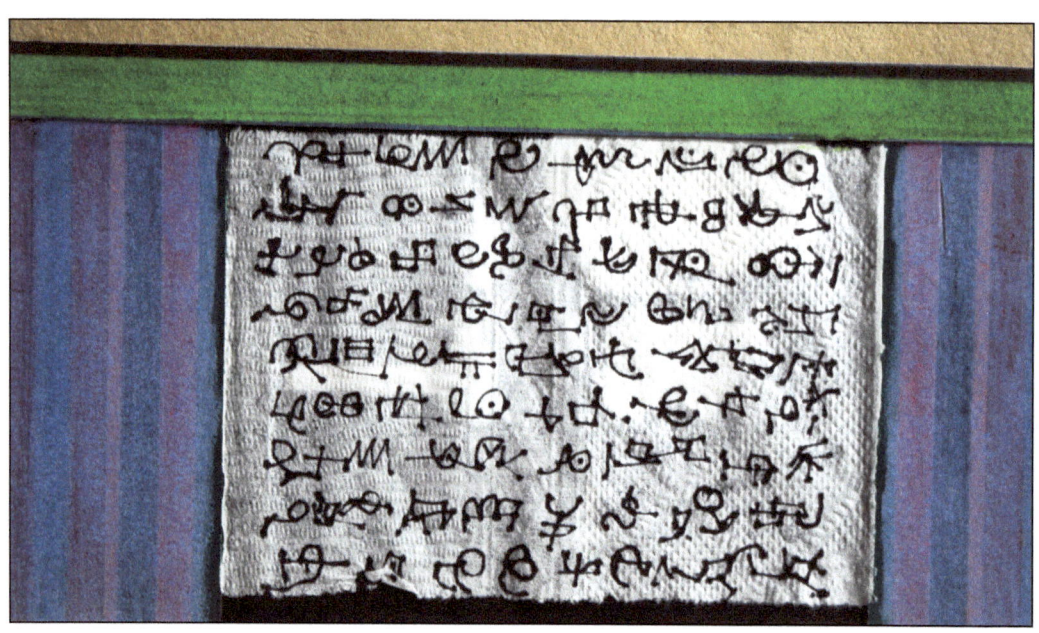

Untitled mixed media collage at right, and close-up above, s.d., 9 3/4x7.5"

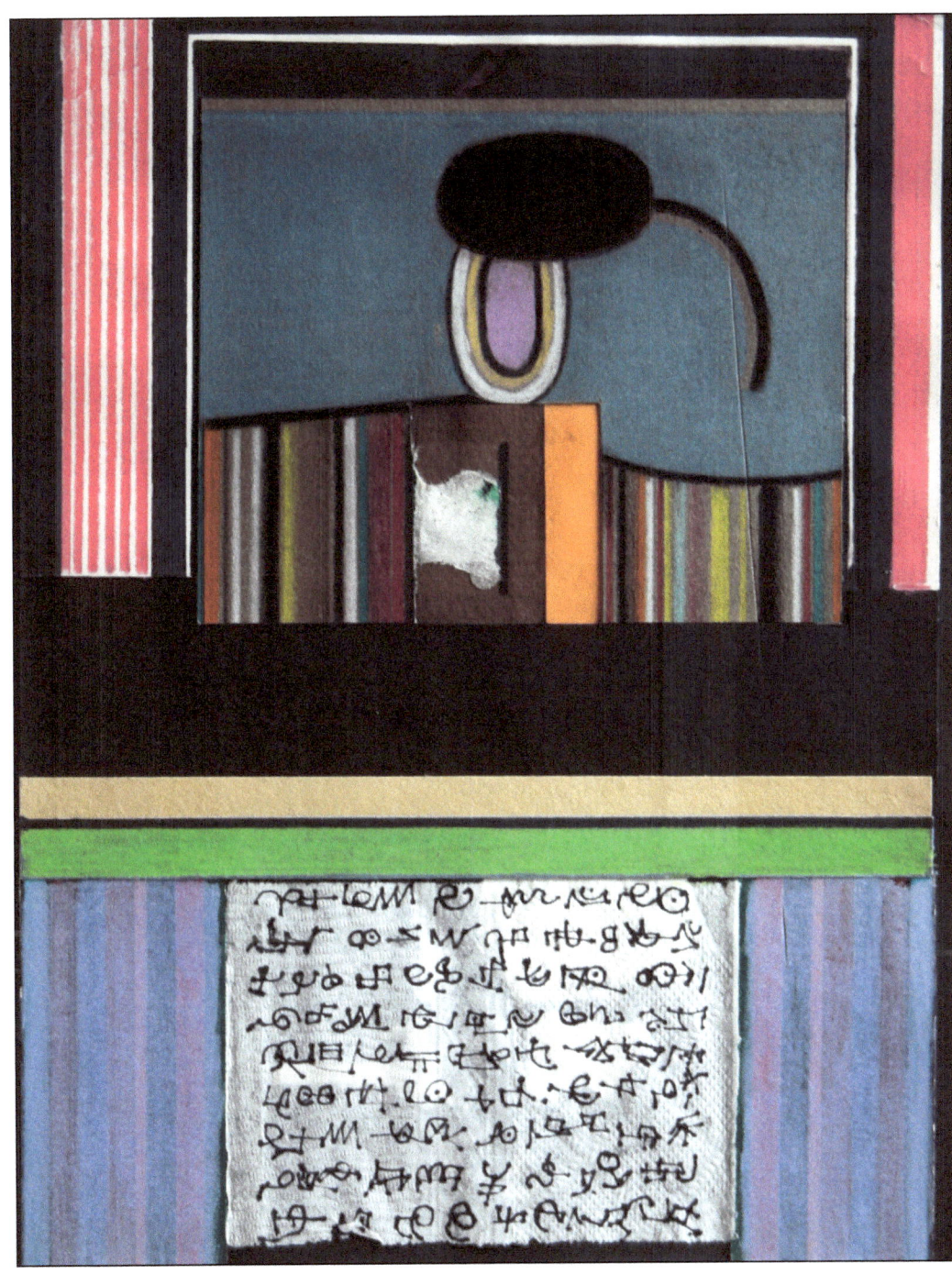

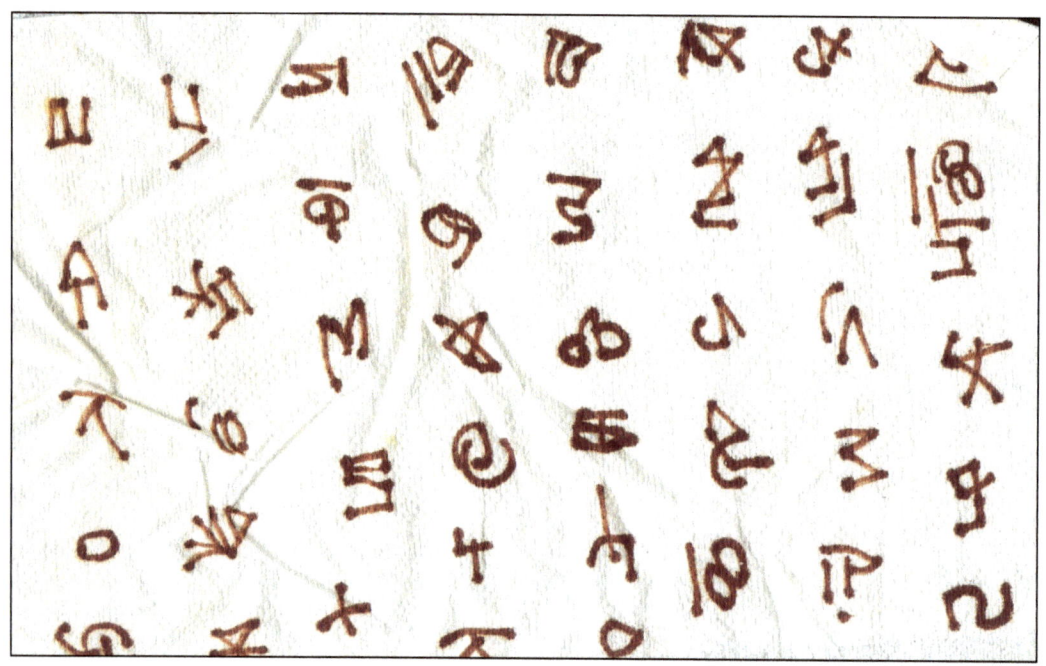

Untitled pen and ink on folded napkin, s.d., 5x3.5"

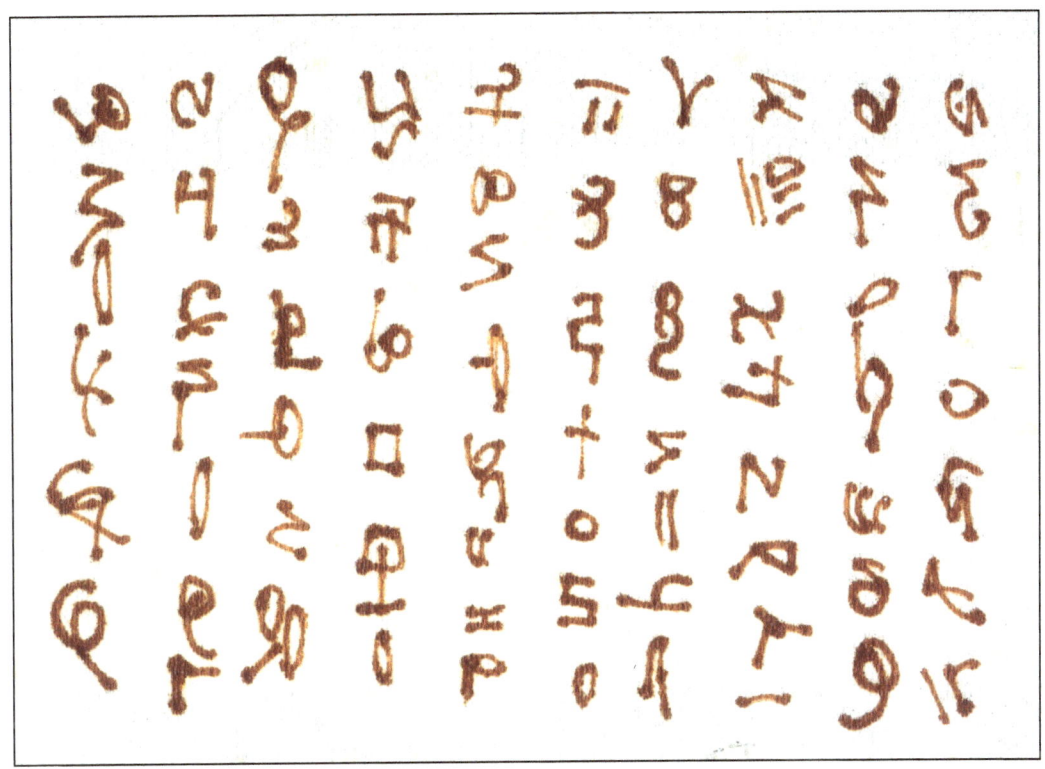

Untitled pen and ink on folded napkin, s.d., 5x3.5"

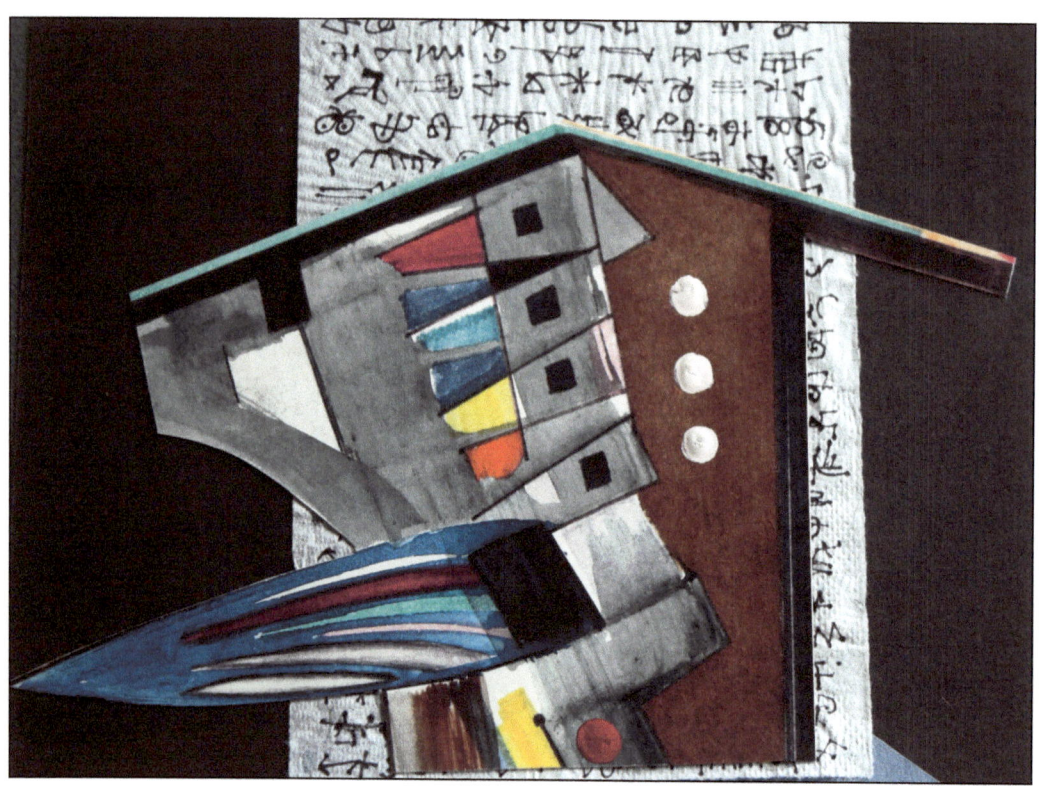

Untitled mixed media collage at right, and close-up above (1983), 14x11"

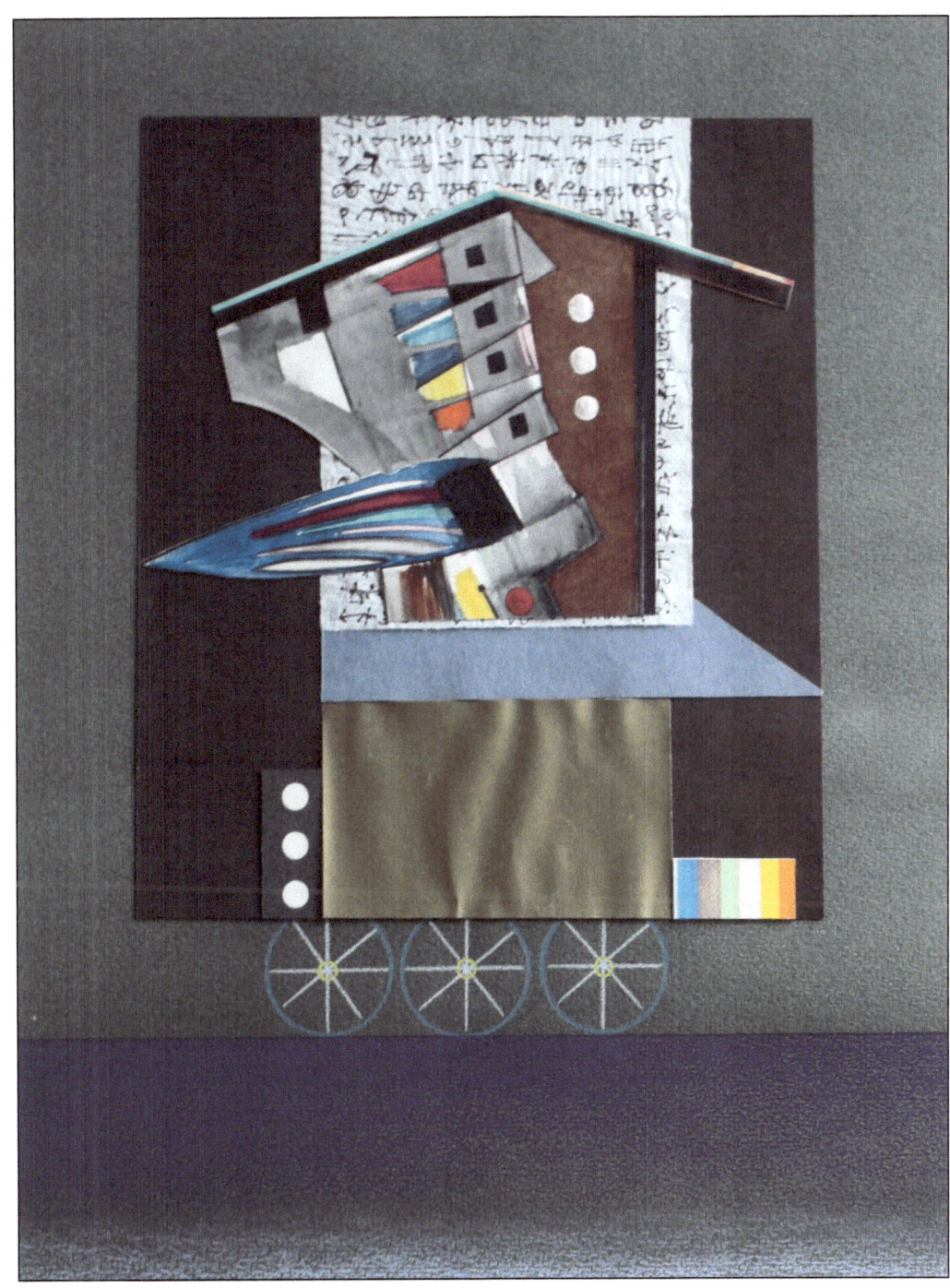

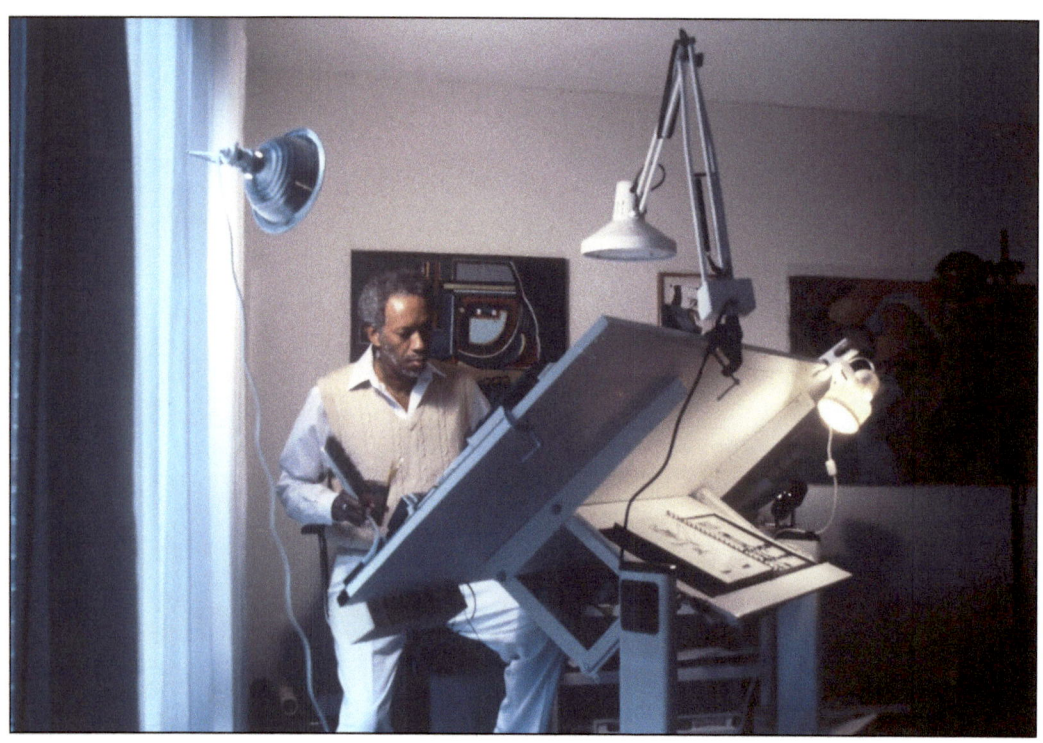

Eugene J. Martin at his desk in his studio in Washington D.C., 1989. During this period he incorporated previously created pen & ink drawings on napkins dating from the 1970' in mixed media collages

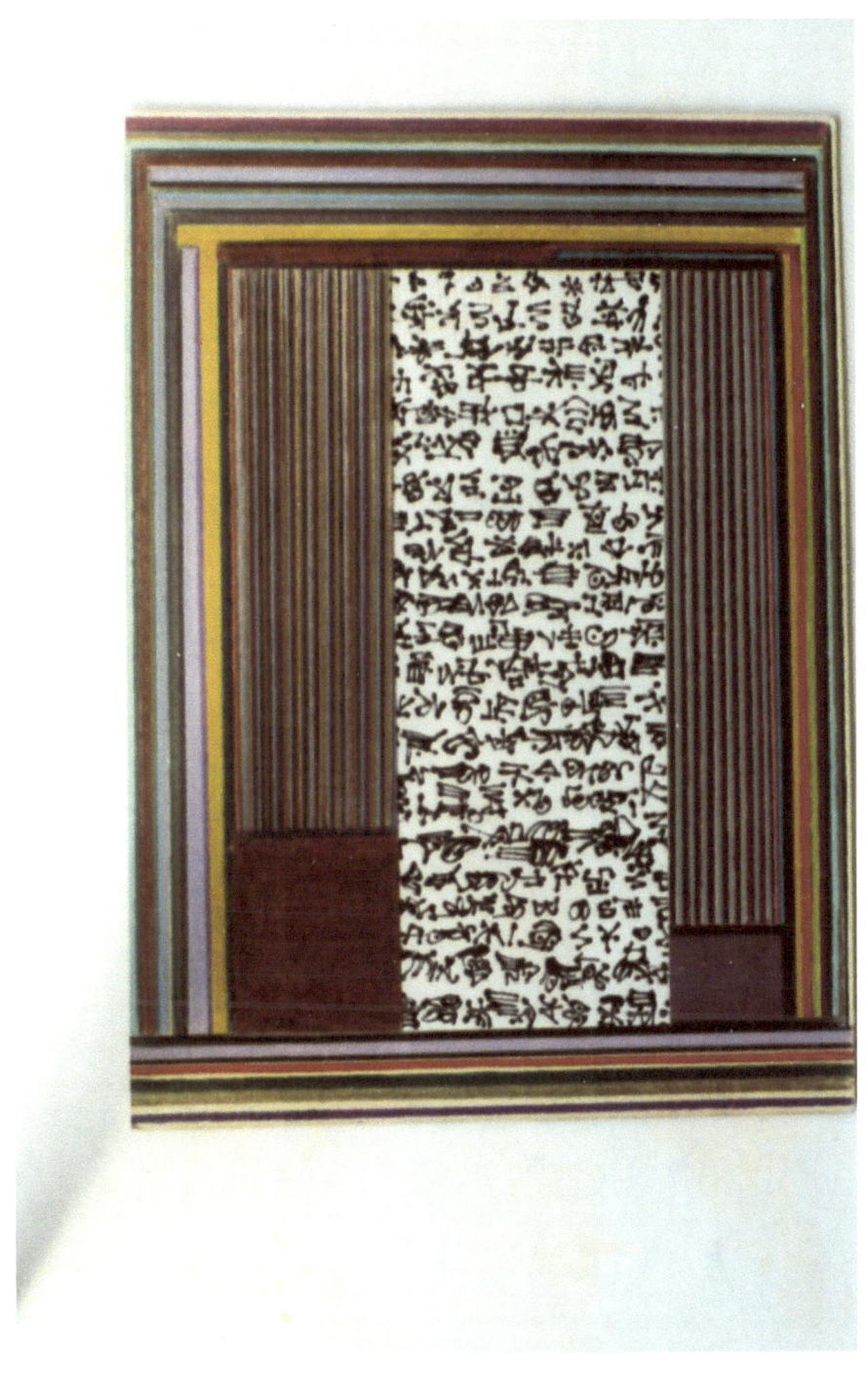

Untitled pen & ink napkin drawing incorporated in framed color pencil drawing, photographed in Washington D.C. in 1988, ~10x8"

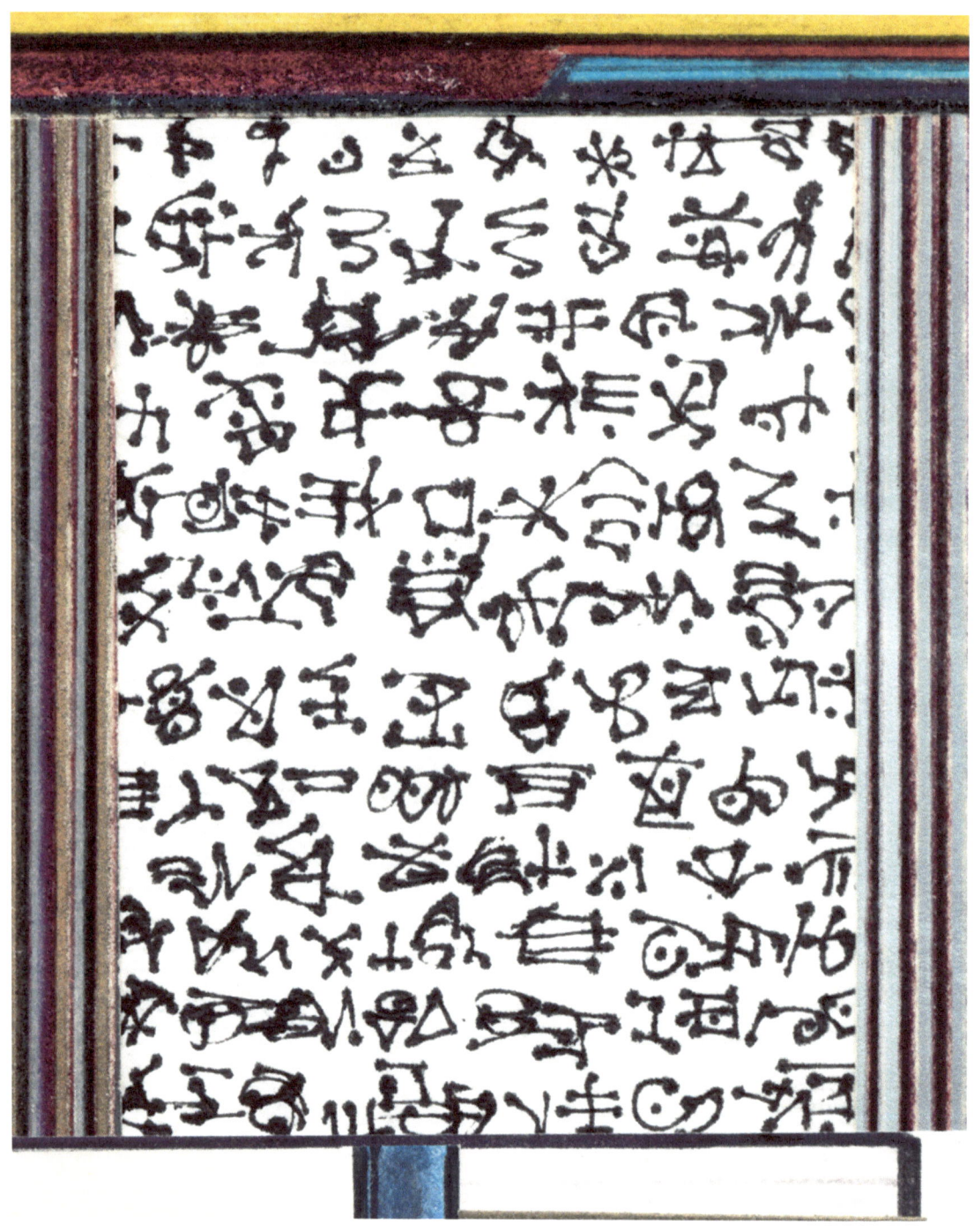

Further incorporation of mixed media drawing into collage shown on preceding page (at right, and close-up above) (1995), photographed in Washington D.C. in 1995, ~10x8"

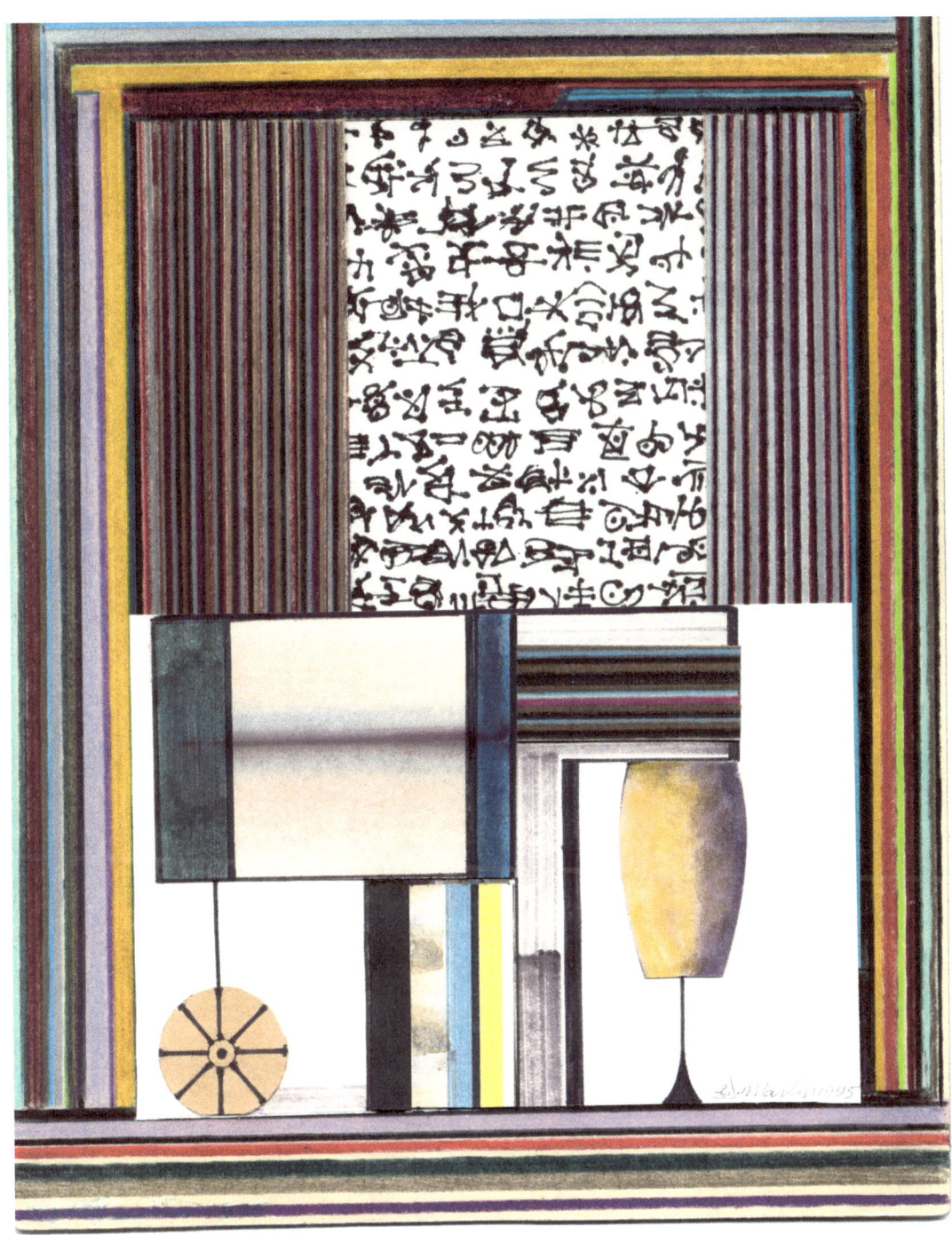

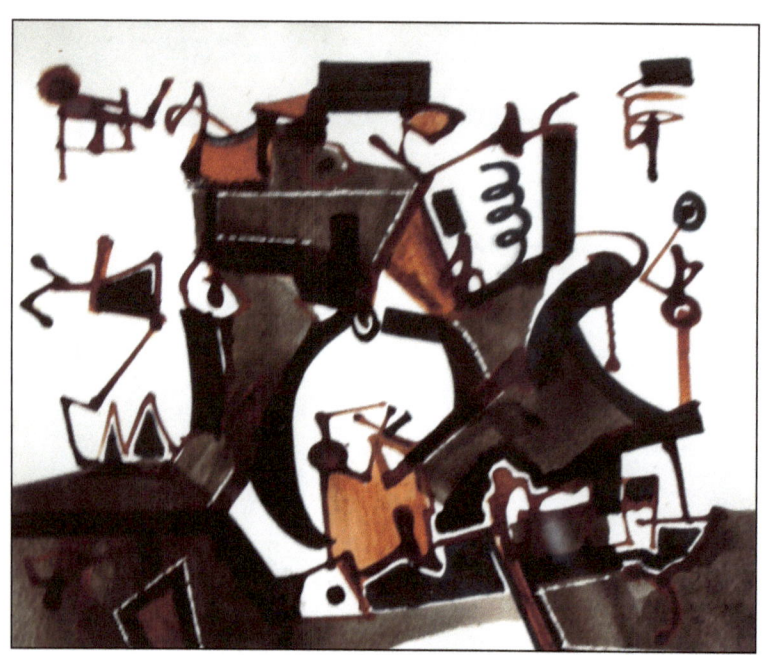

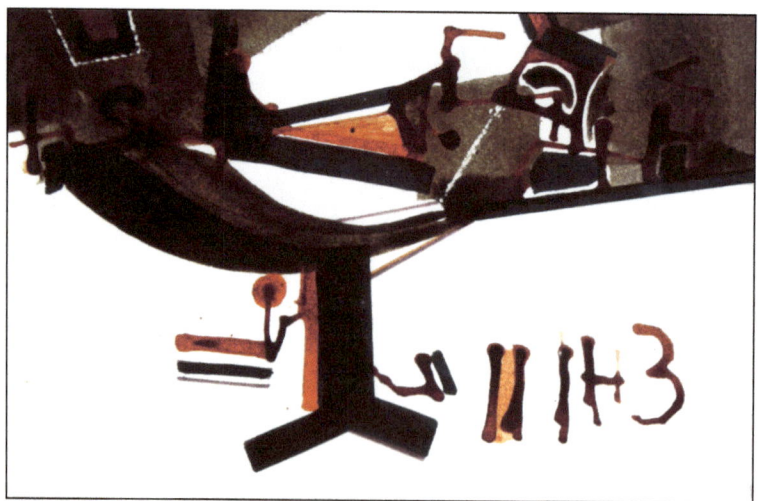

Untitled pen and ink at right, and close-up above, 1981,~10x7"

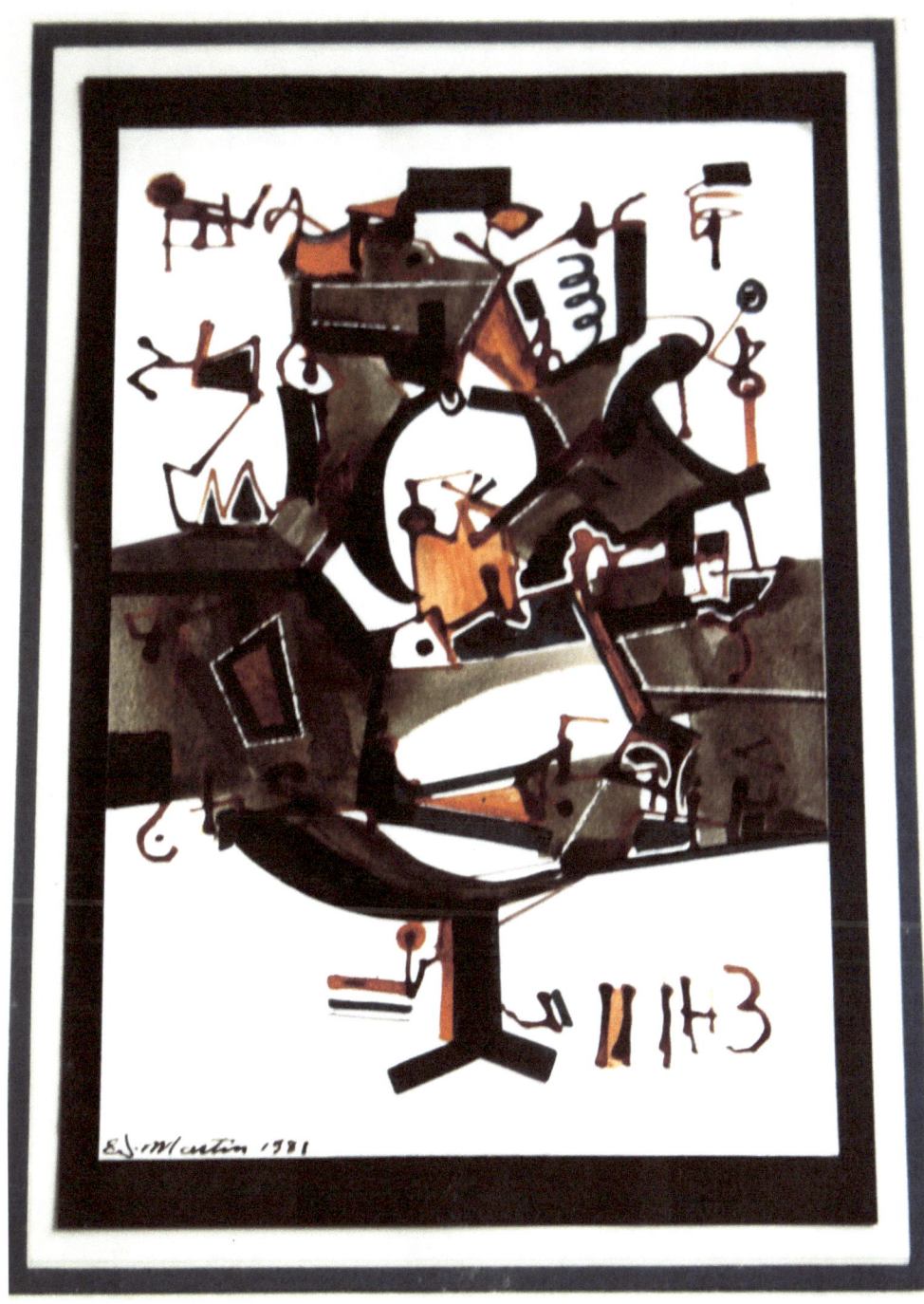

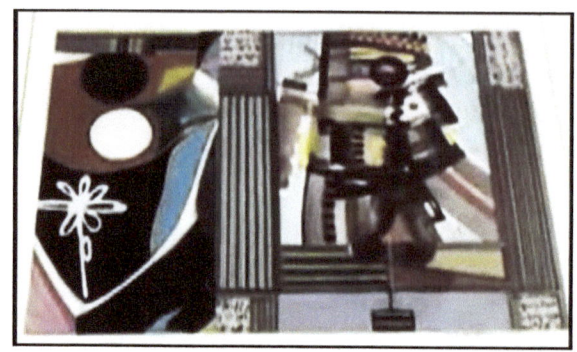

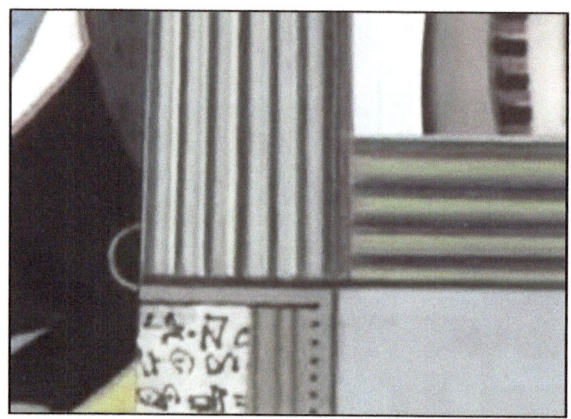

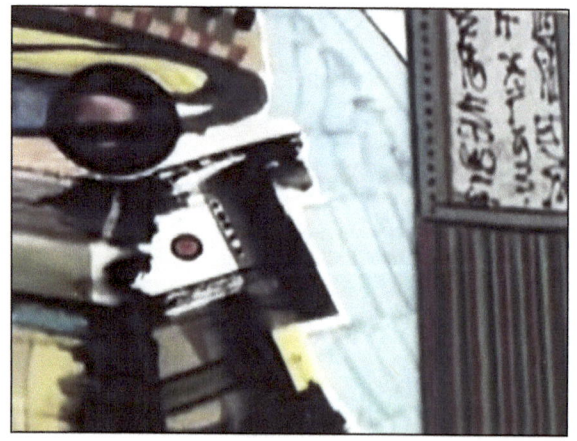

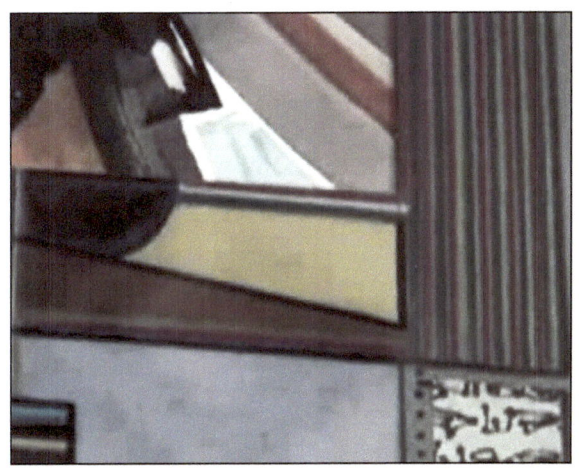

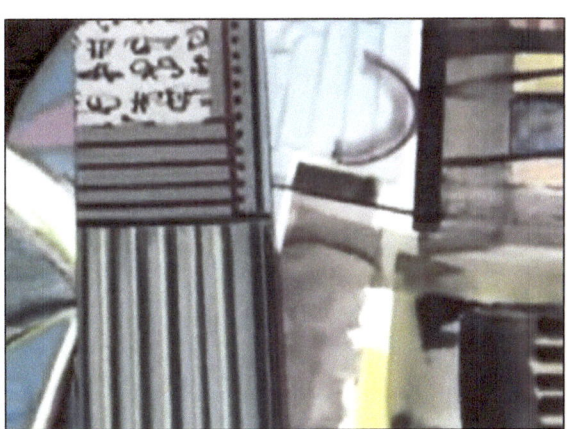

Untitled mixed media collage at upper left; close-up at center left and lower left, and above, s.d., (1970's), ~13x9"

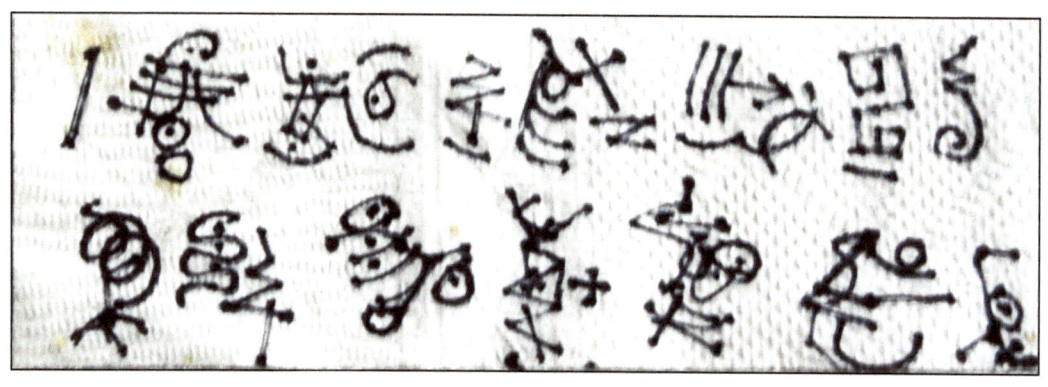

Annotated drawing with Eugene Martin quote (1970')''at right, and close-up above, 9.5x6.5''

"TRUTH RIDES BEST
IN THAT WHICH
LOOKS RIDICULOUS."

E. J. MARTIN

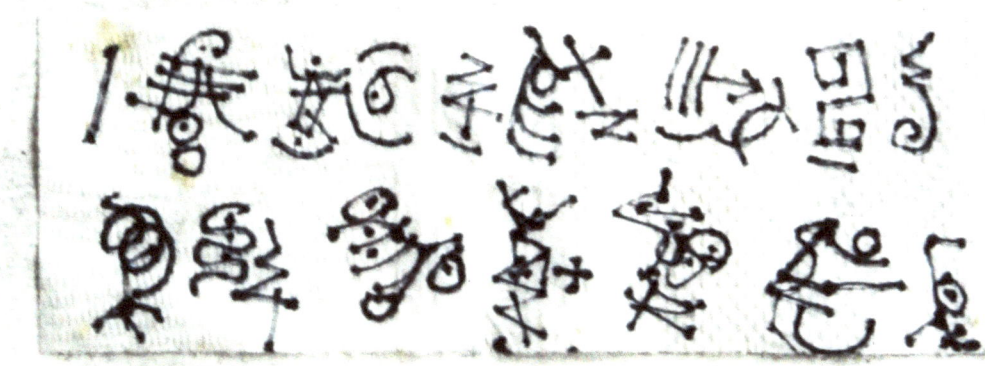

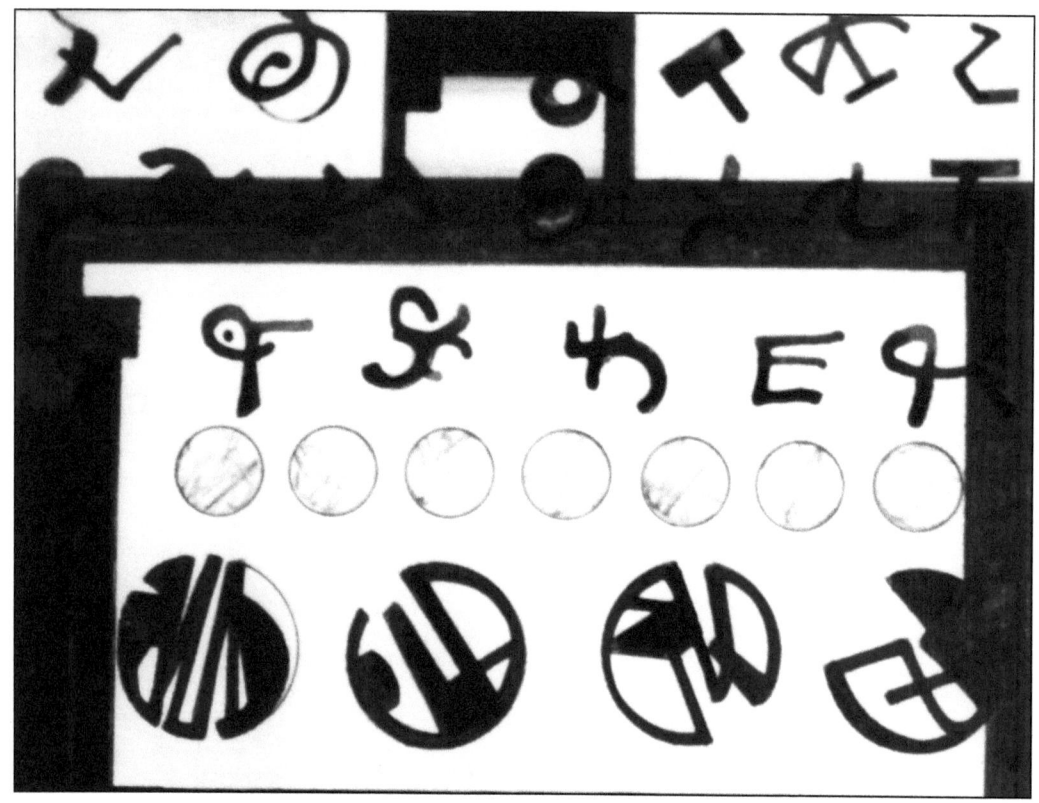

Untitled mixed media collage at right, and close-up above (1997), 11.5x7.5"

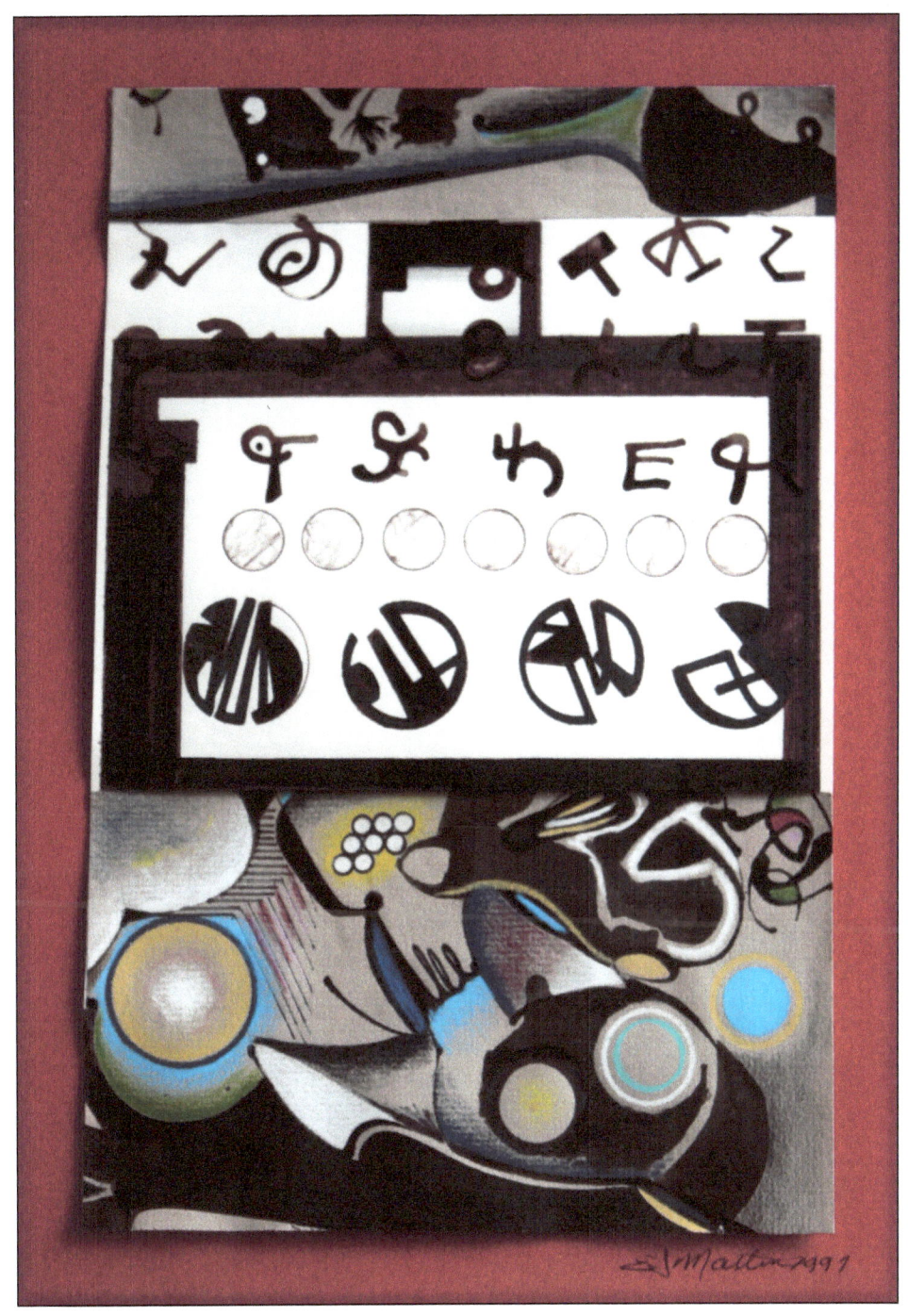

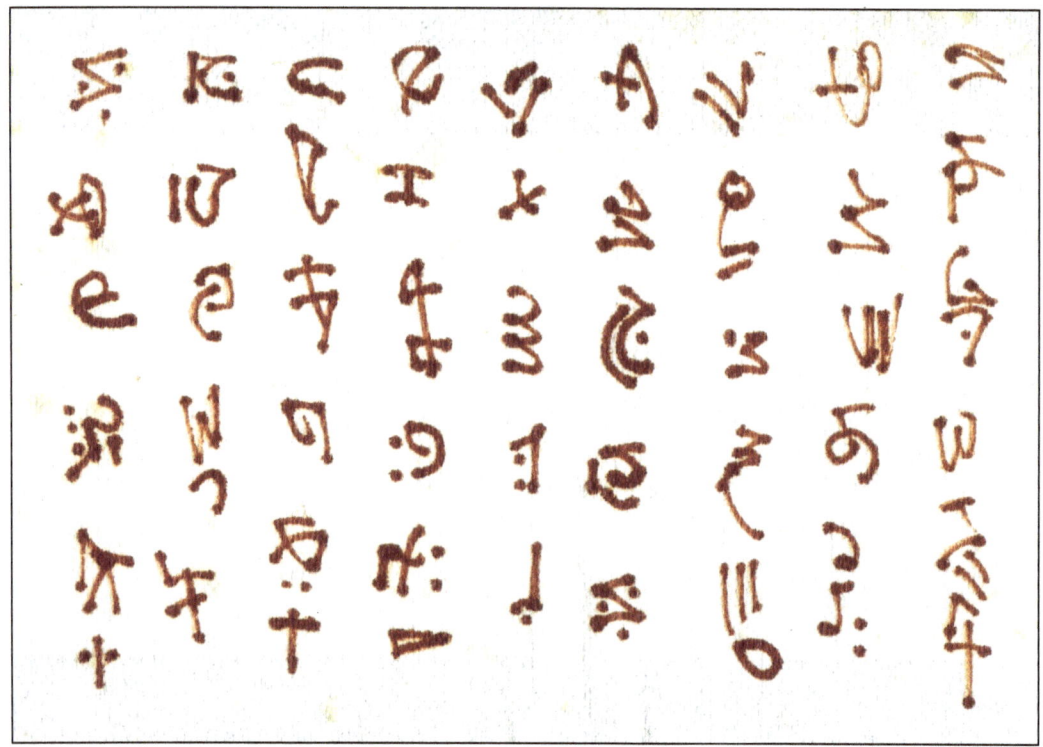

Untitled pen and ink on folded napkin, s.d., 5x3.5"

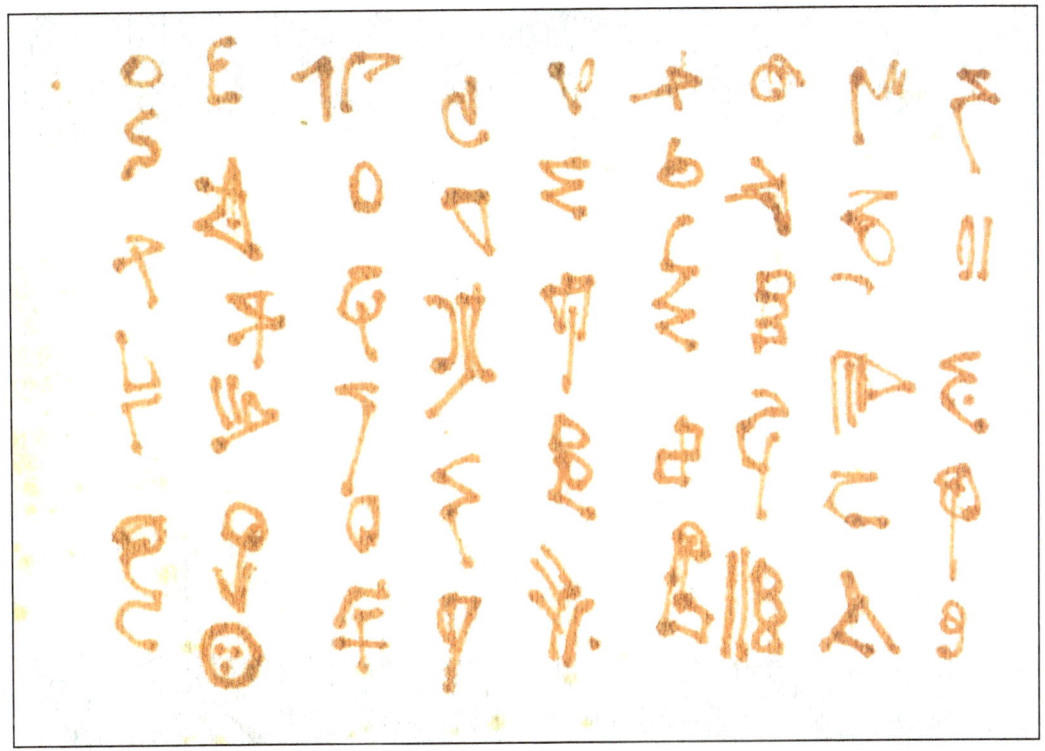

Untitled pen and ink on folded napkin, s.d., 5x3.5"

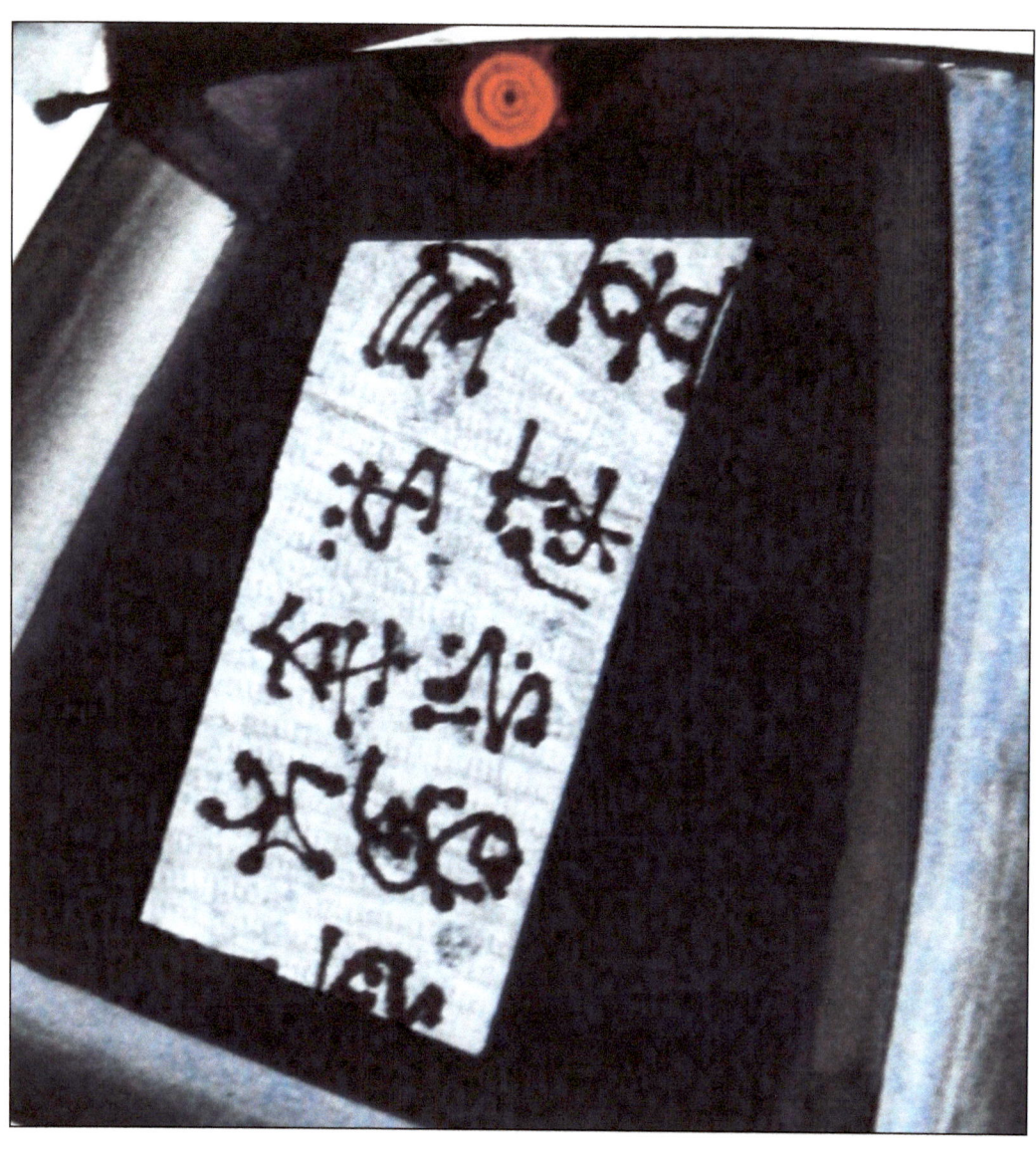

Untitled mixed media collage at right, and close-up above (1974-1980), 9x6 1/4"

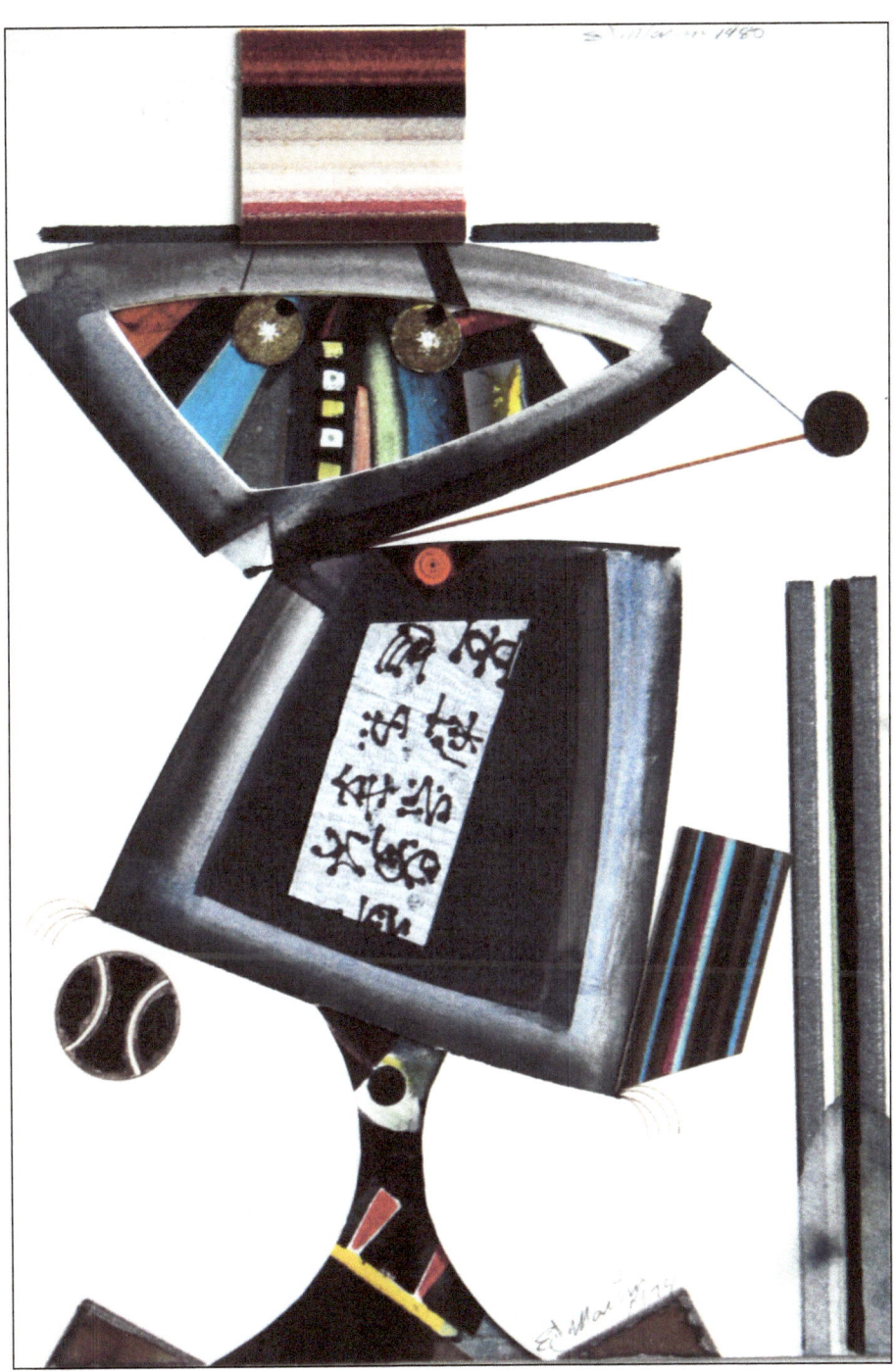

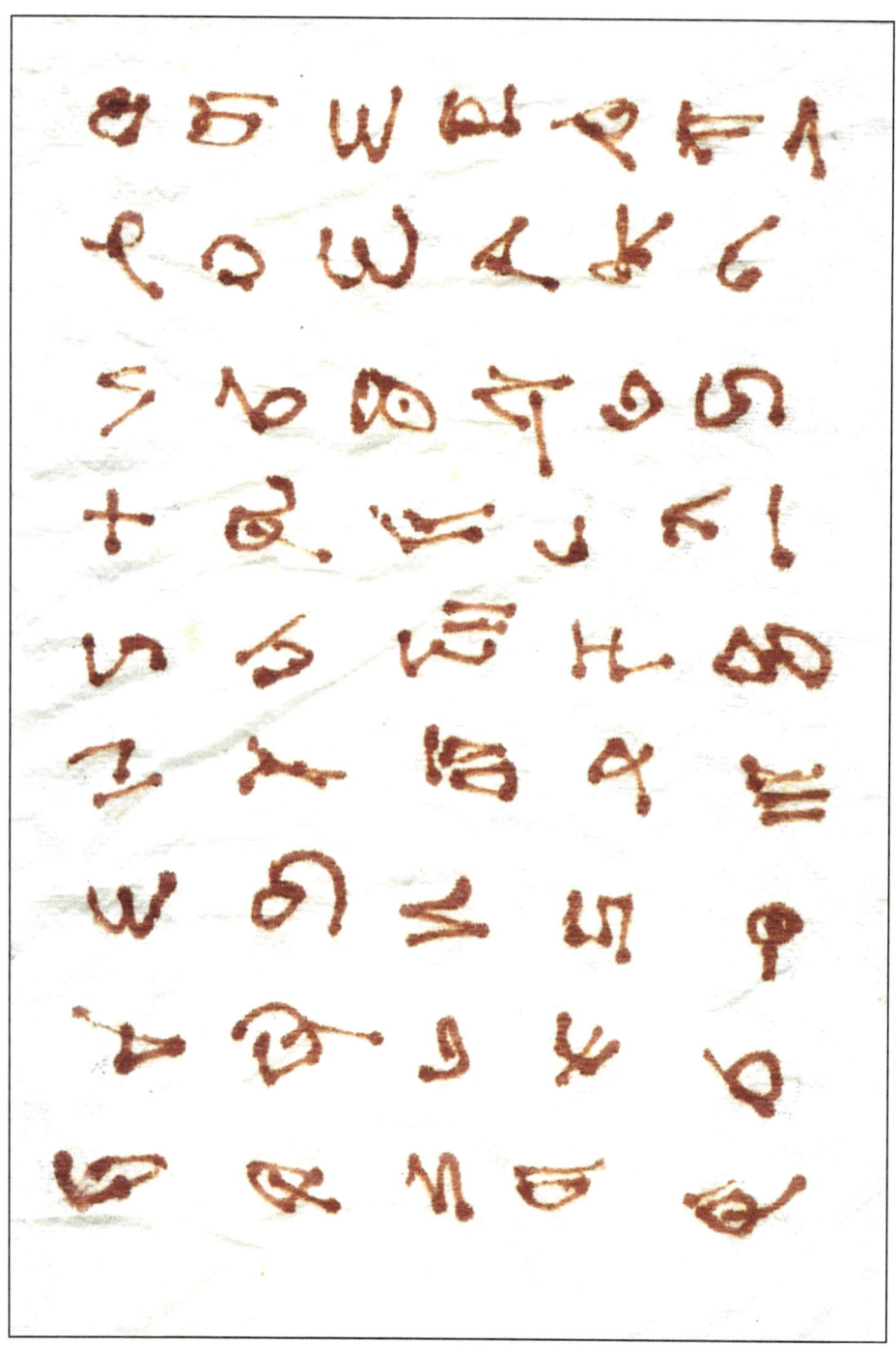

Untitled pen and ink on folded napkin, s.d., 5x3.5"

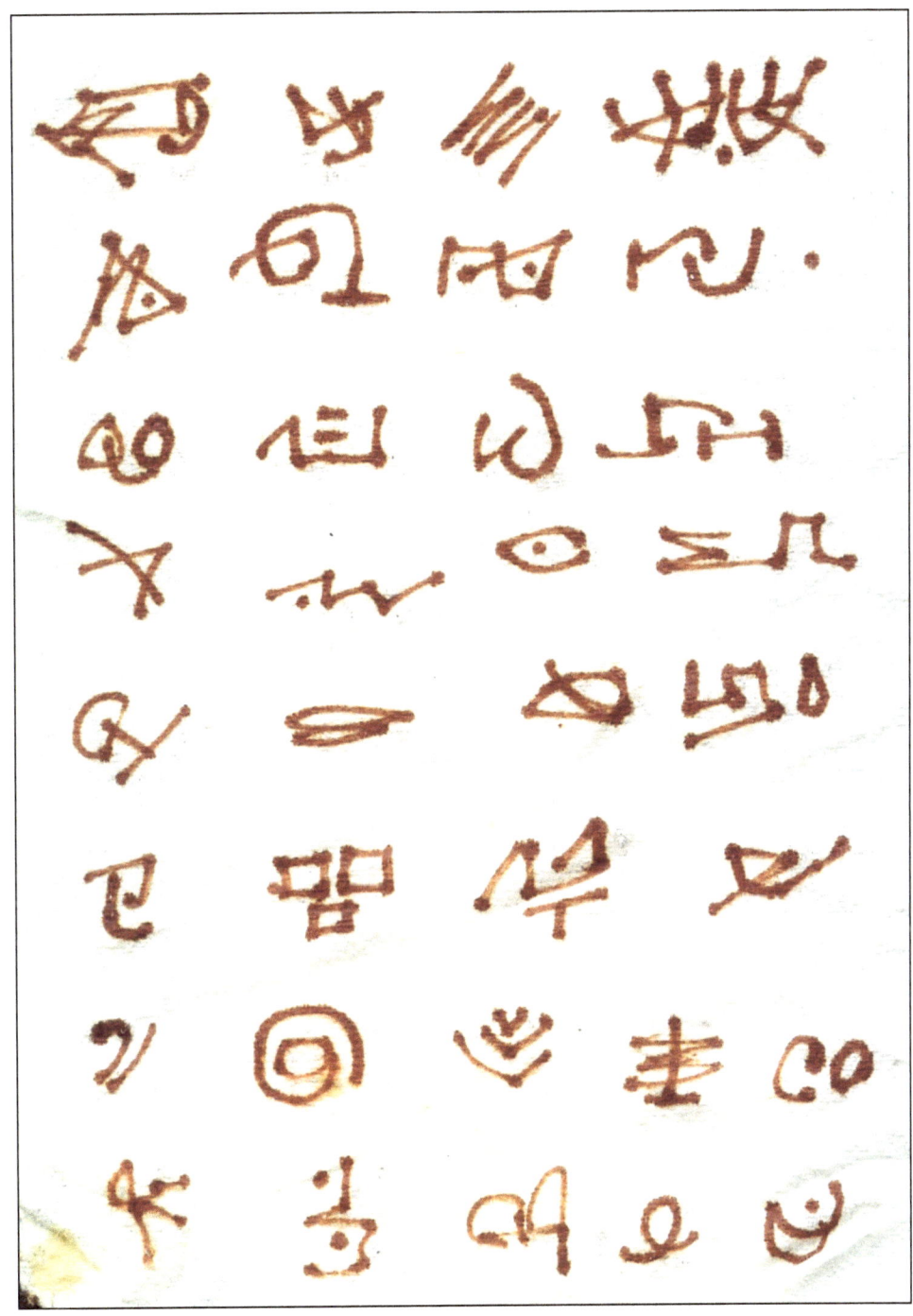

Untitled pen and ink on folded napkin, s.d., 5x3.5"

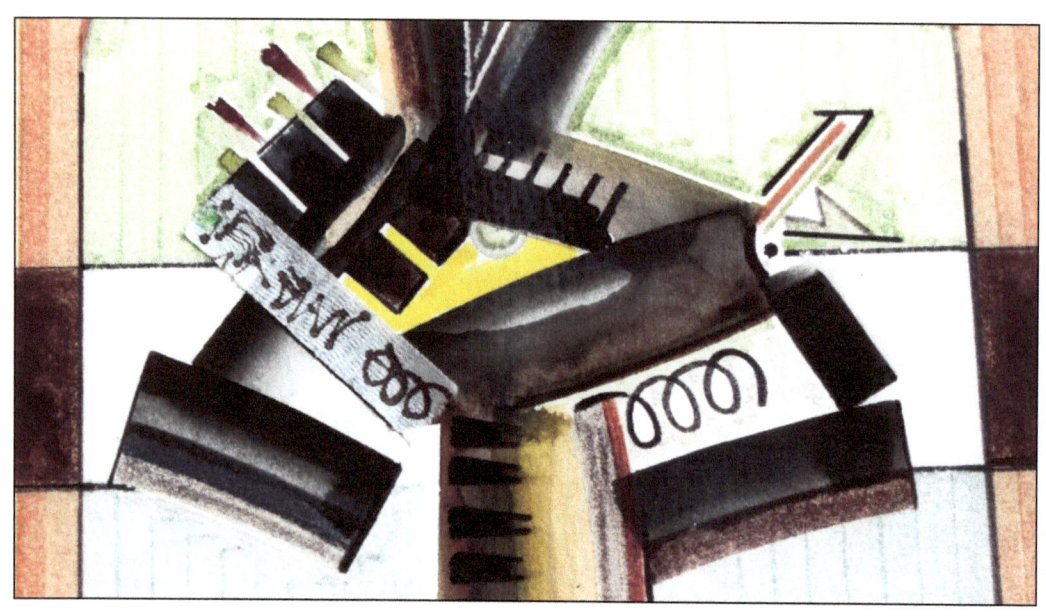

Untitled mixed media collage at right, and close-up above (1974-1997), 17x12"

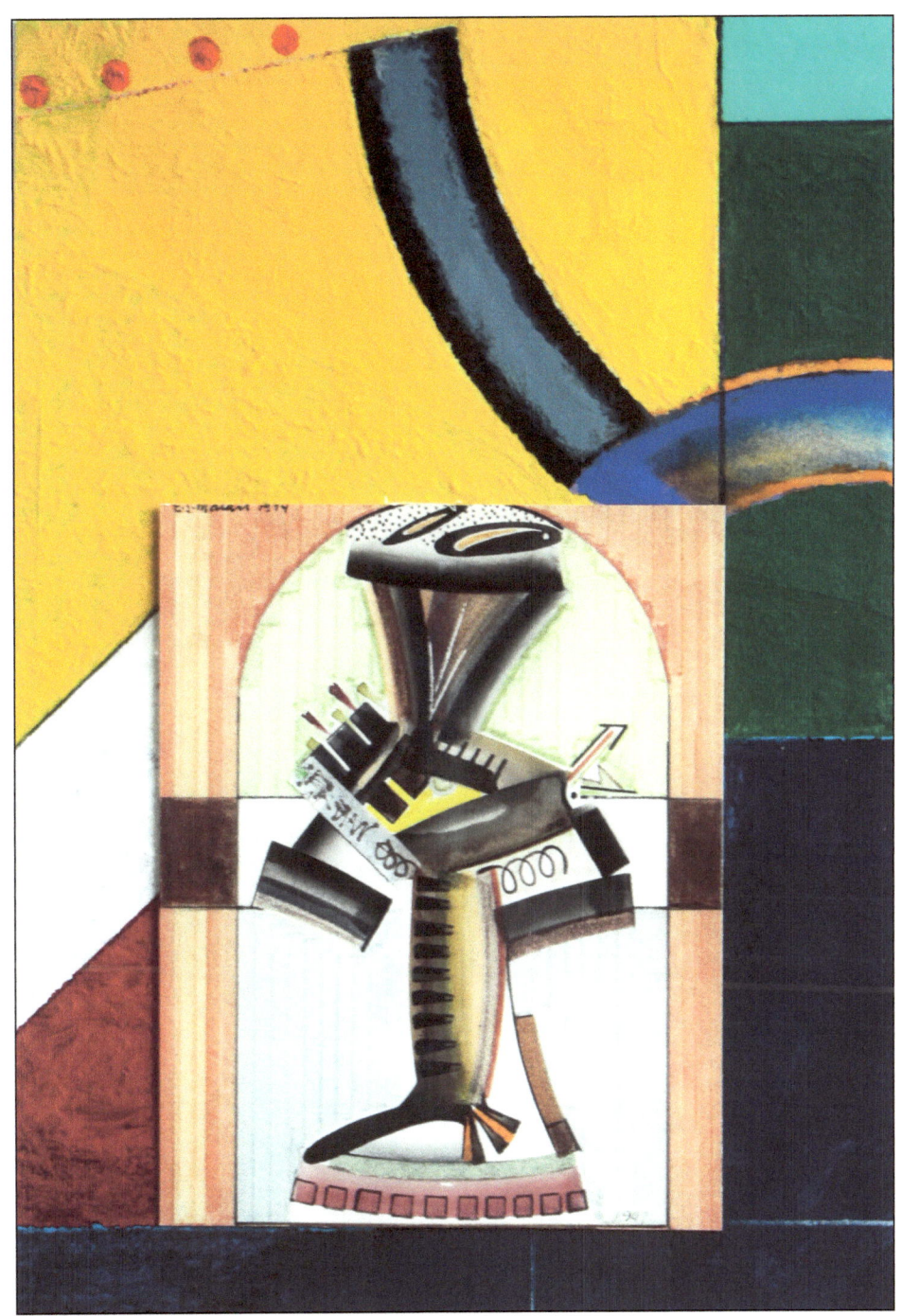

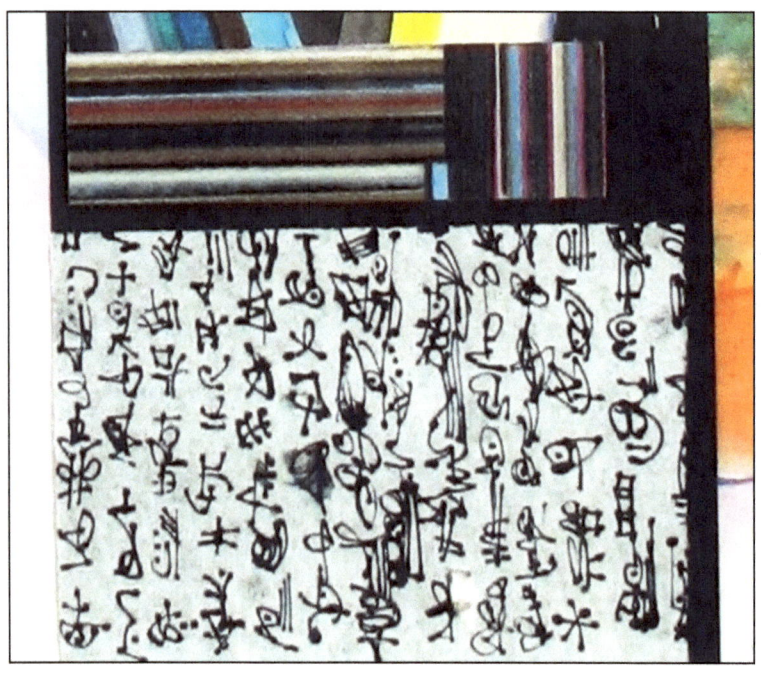

Untitled mixed media collage at right, and close-up above (1997), 15.5x11"

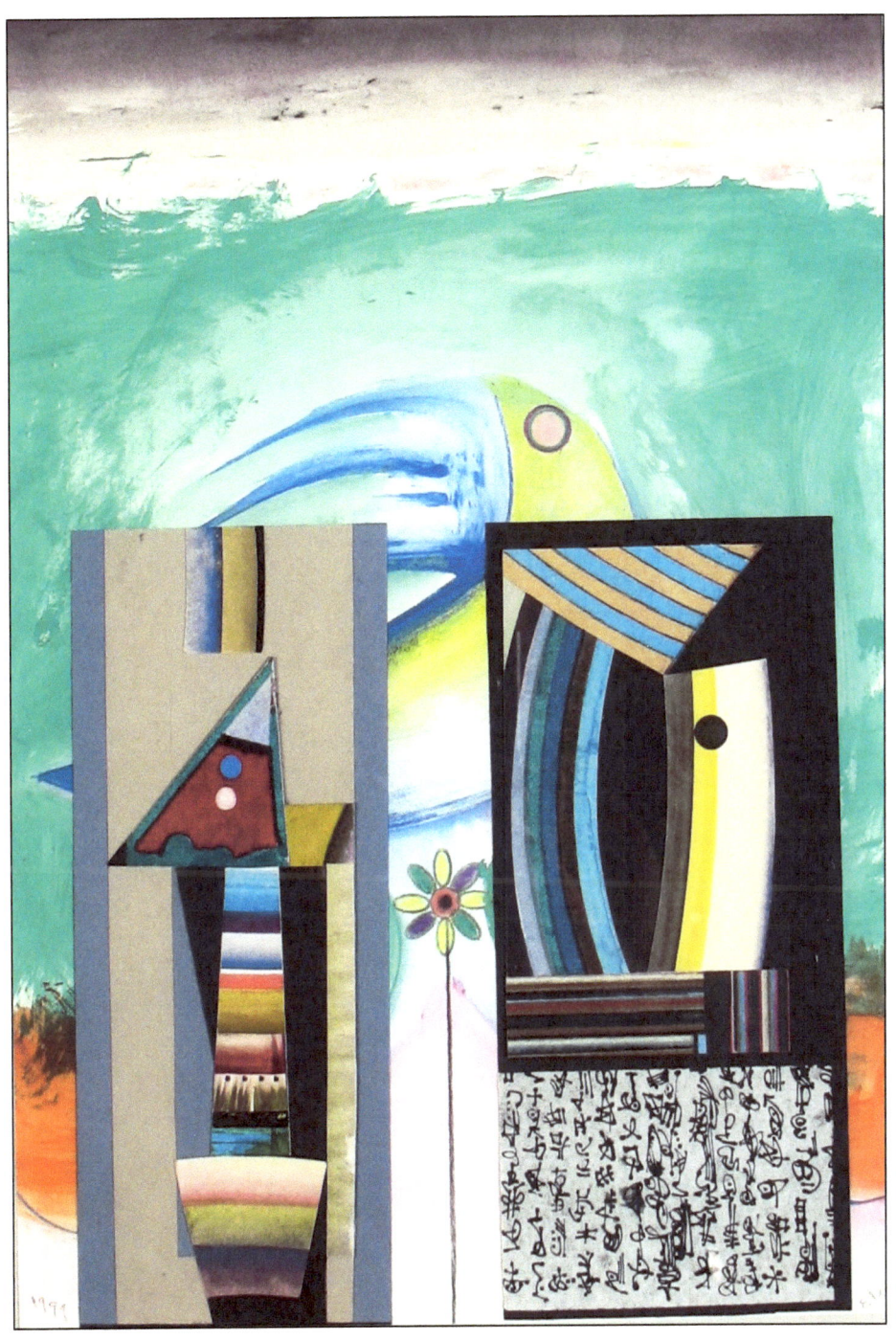

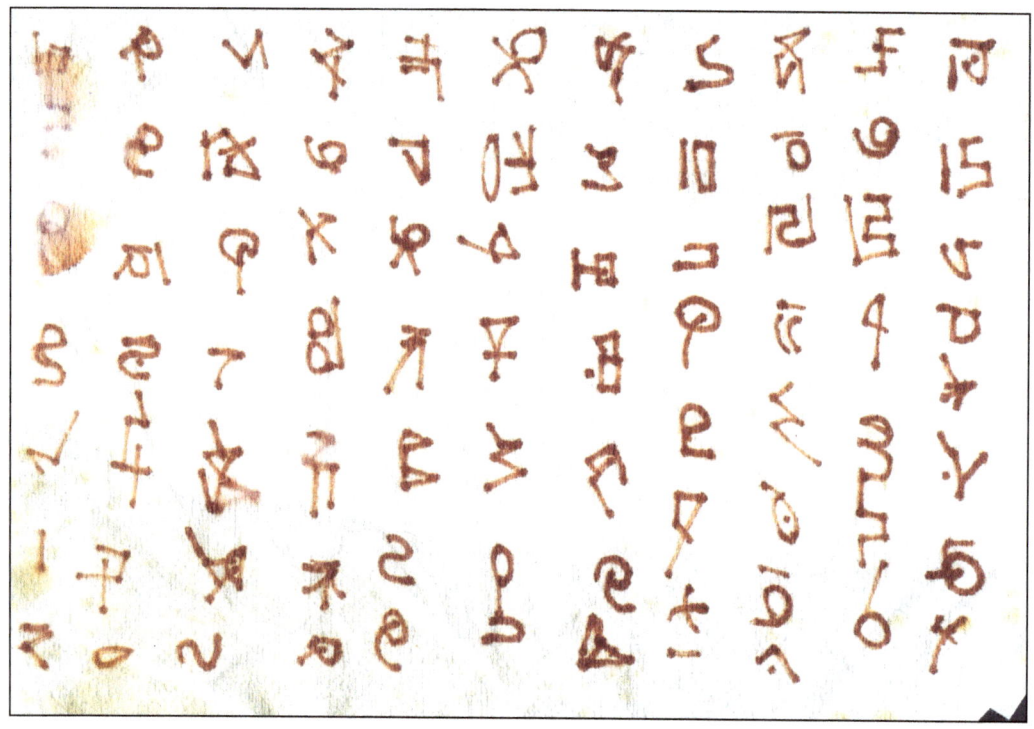

Untitled pen and ink on folded napkin, s.d., 5x3.5"

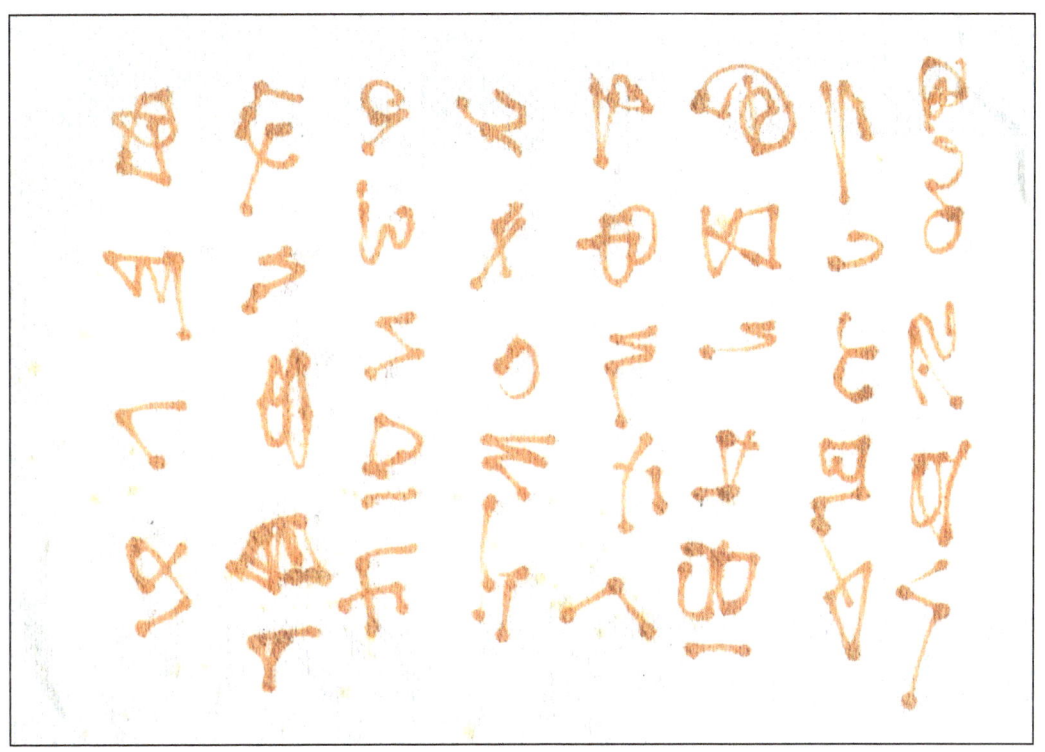

Untitled pen and ink on folded napkin, s.d., 5x3.5"

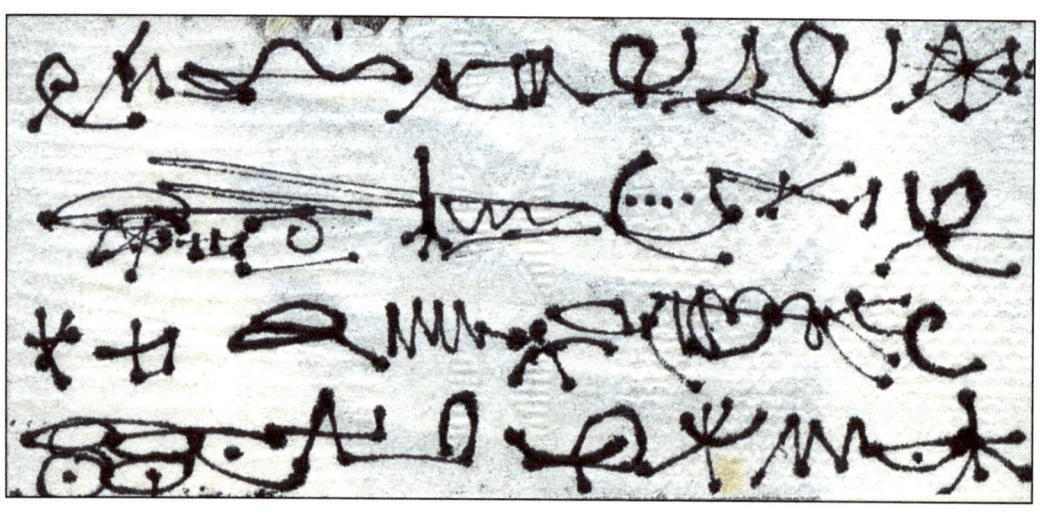

Napkin fragment (above) incorporated in untitled 1978 graphite drawing on paper, 9.5x6.1/4" (at right)

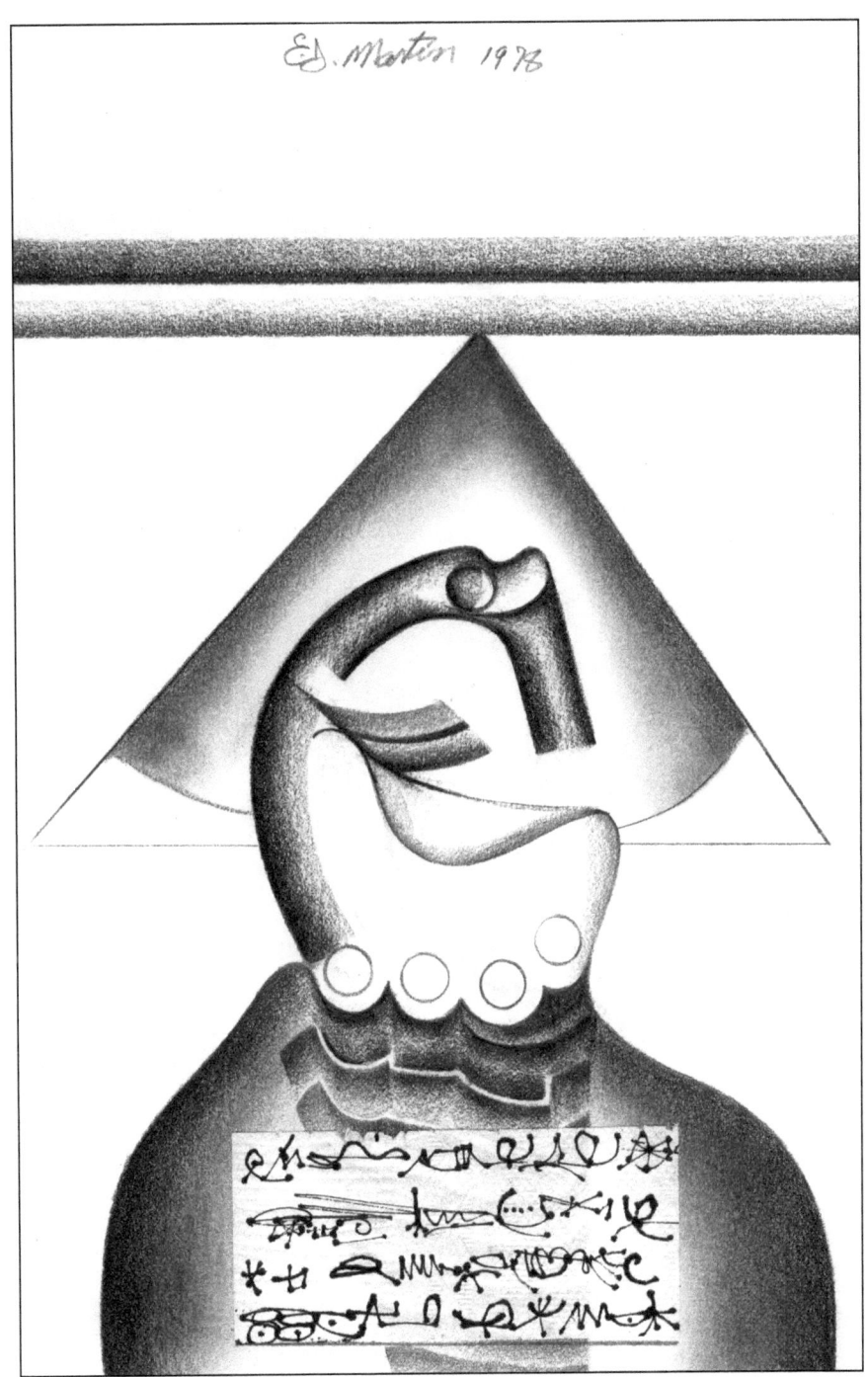

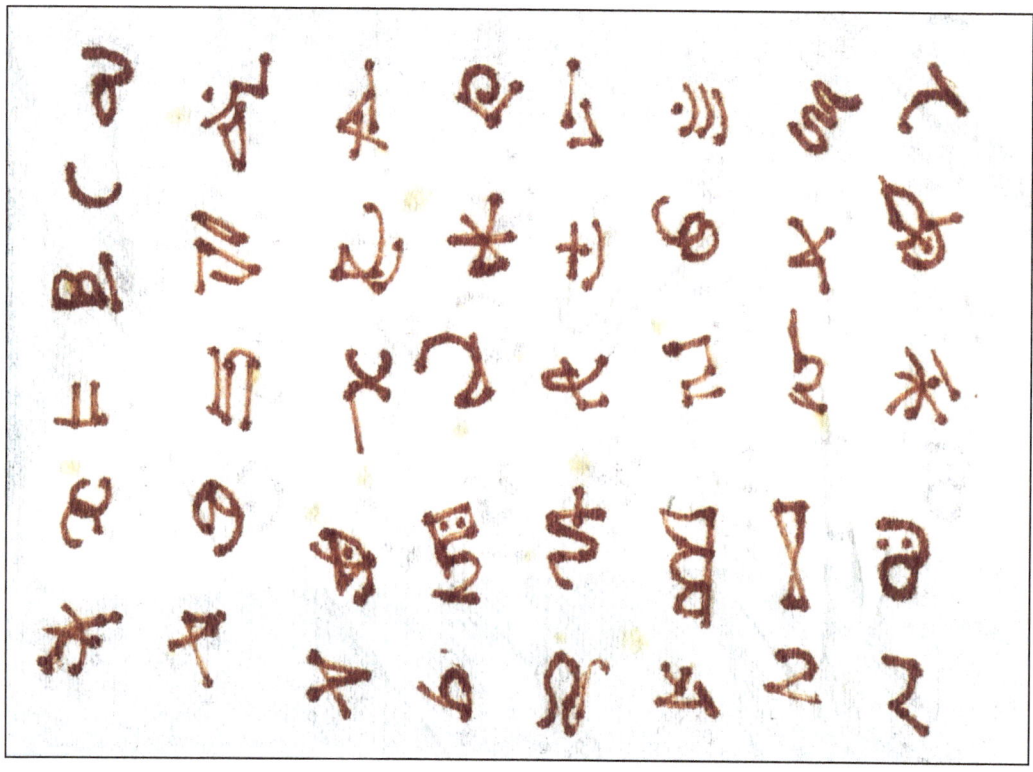

Untitled pen and ink on folded napkin, s.d., 3.5x5"

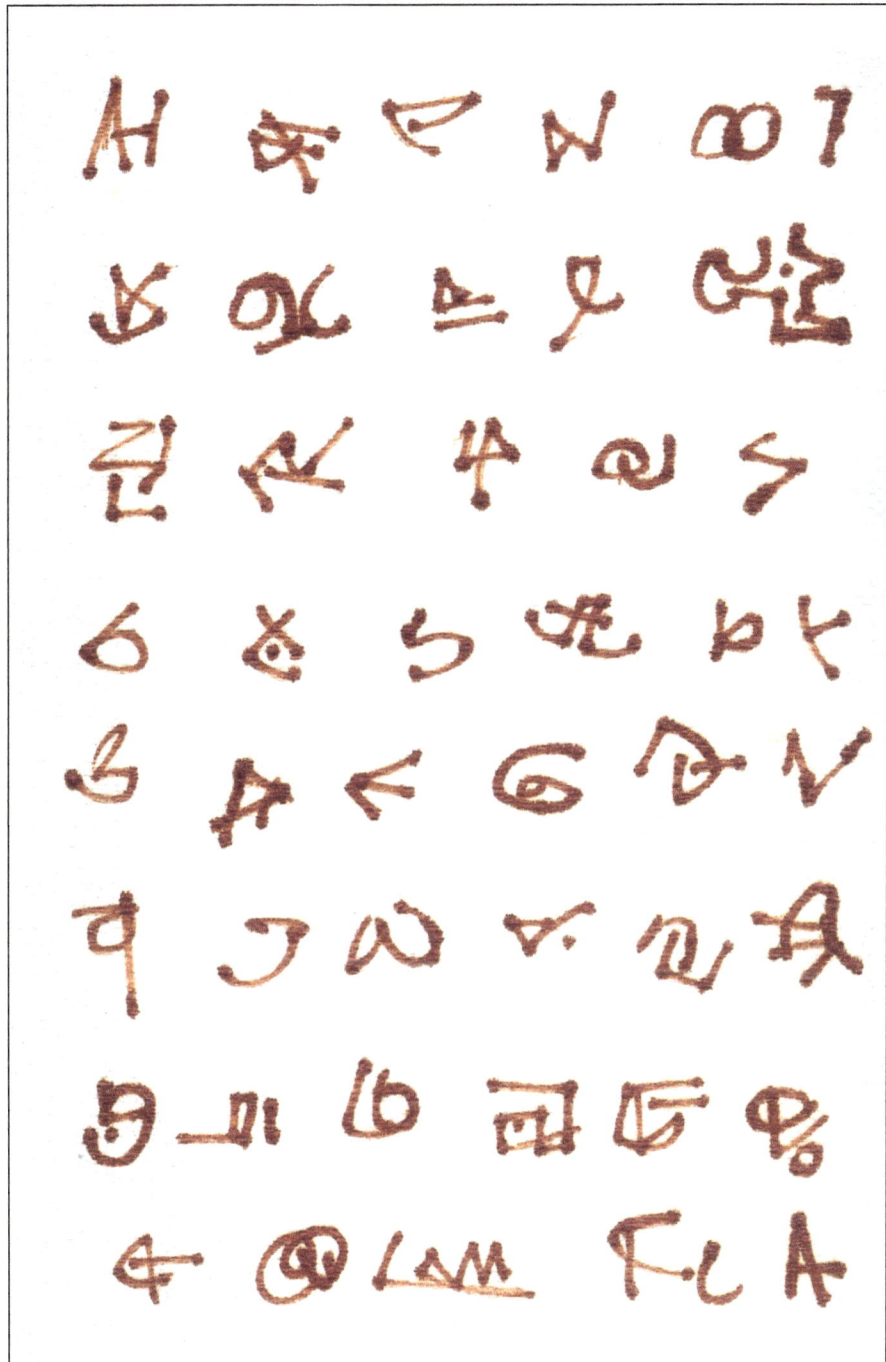

Untitled pen and ink on folded napkin, s.d., 5x3.5"

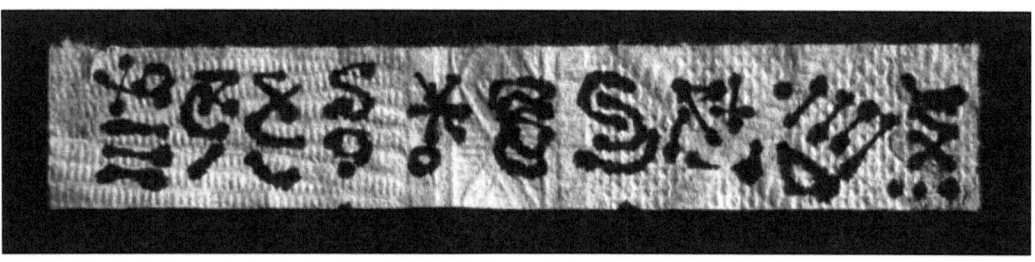

Untitled mixed media collage at right, and close-up above (1999), 12.5x8"

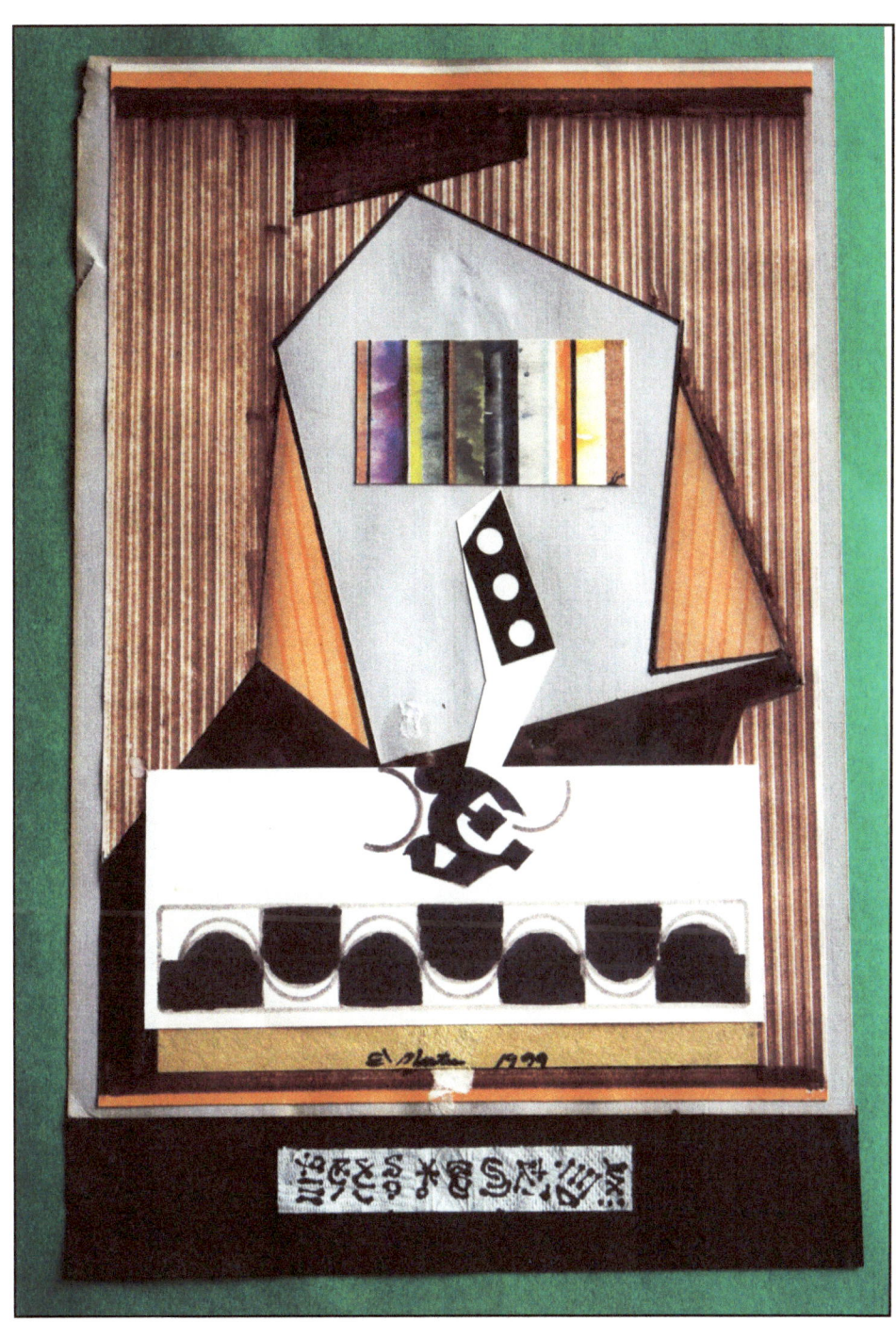

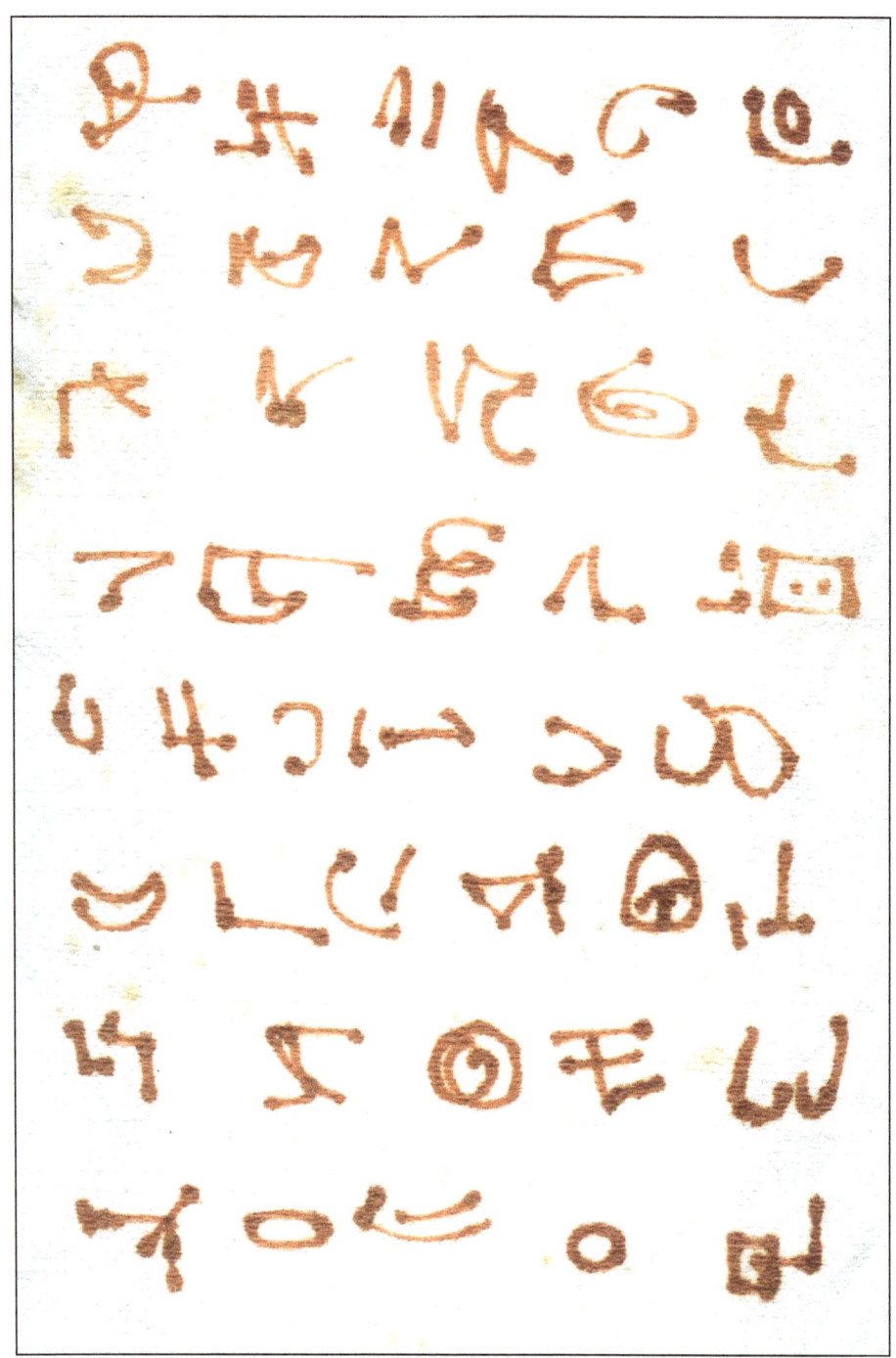

Untitled pen and ink on folded napkin, s.d., 5x3.5"

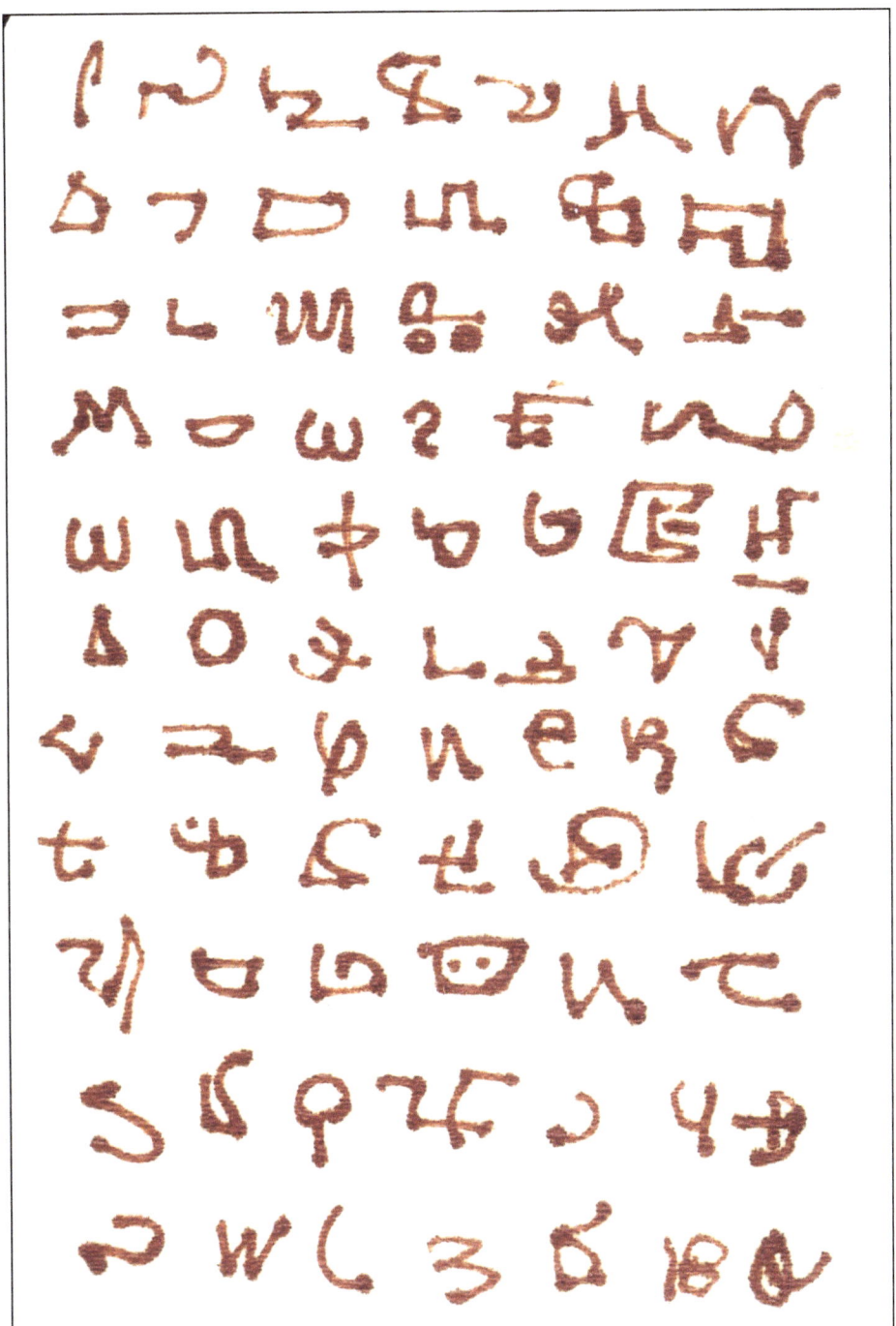

Untitled pen and ink on folded napkin, s.d., 5x3.5"

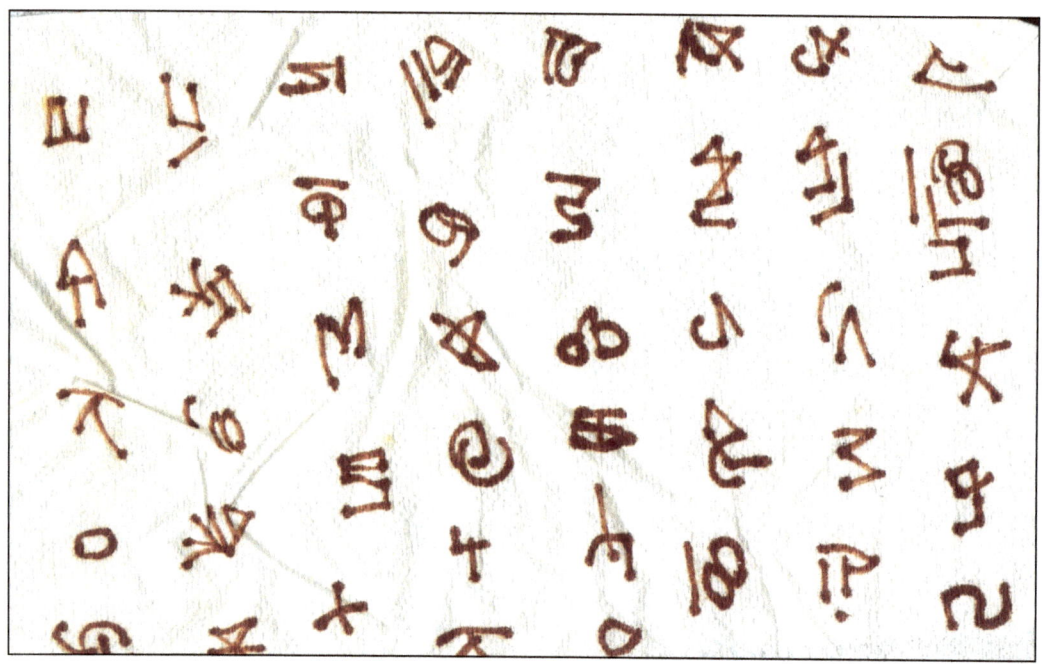

Untitled pen and ink on folded napkin, s.d. 3.5x5"

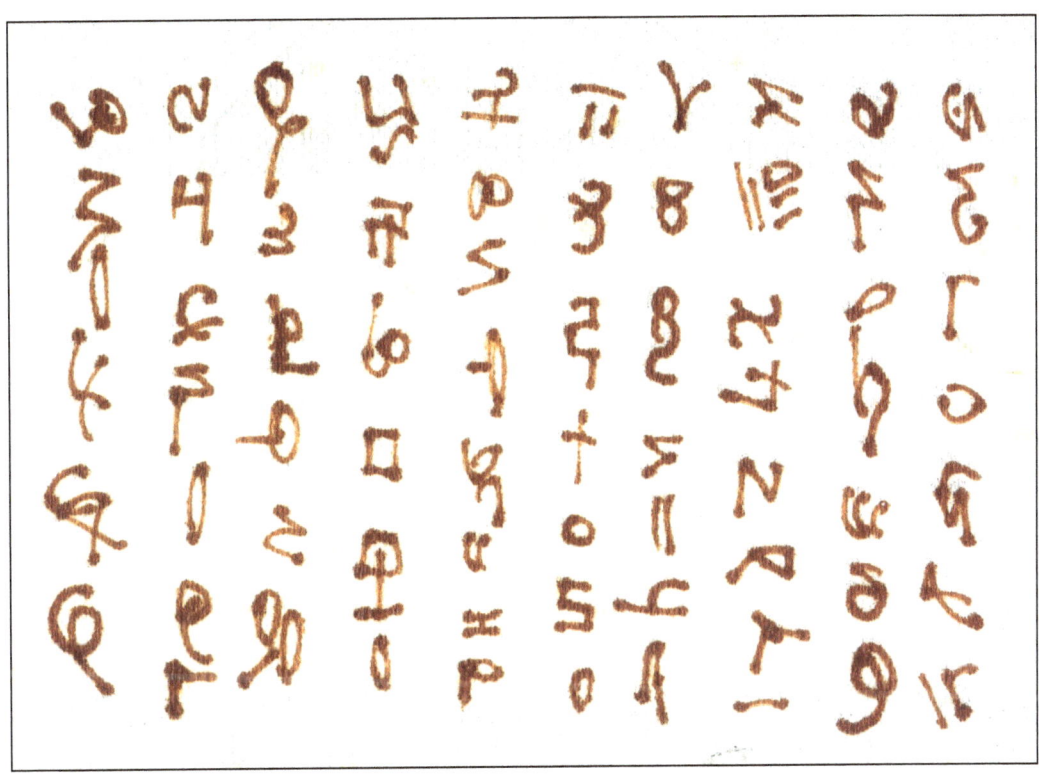

Untitled pen and ink on folded napkin, s.d., 5x3.5"

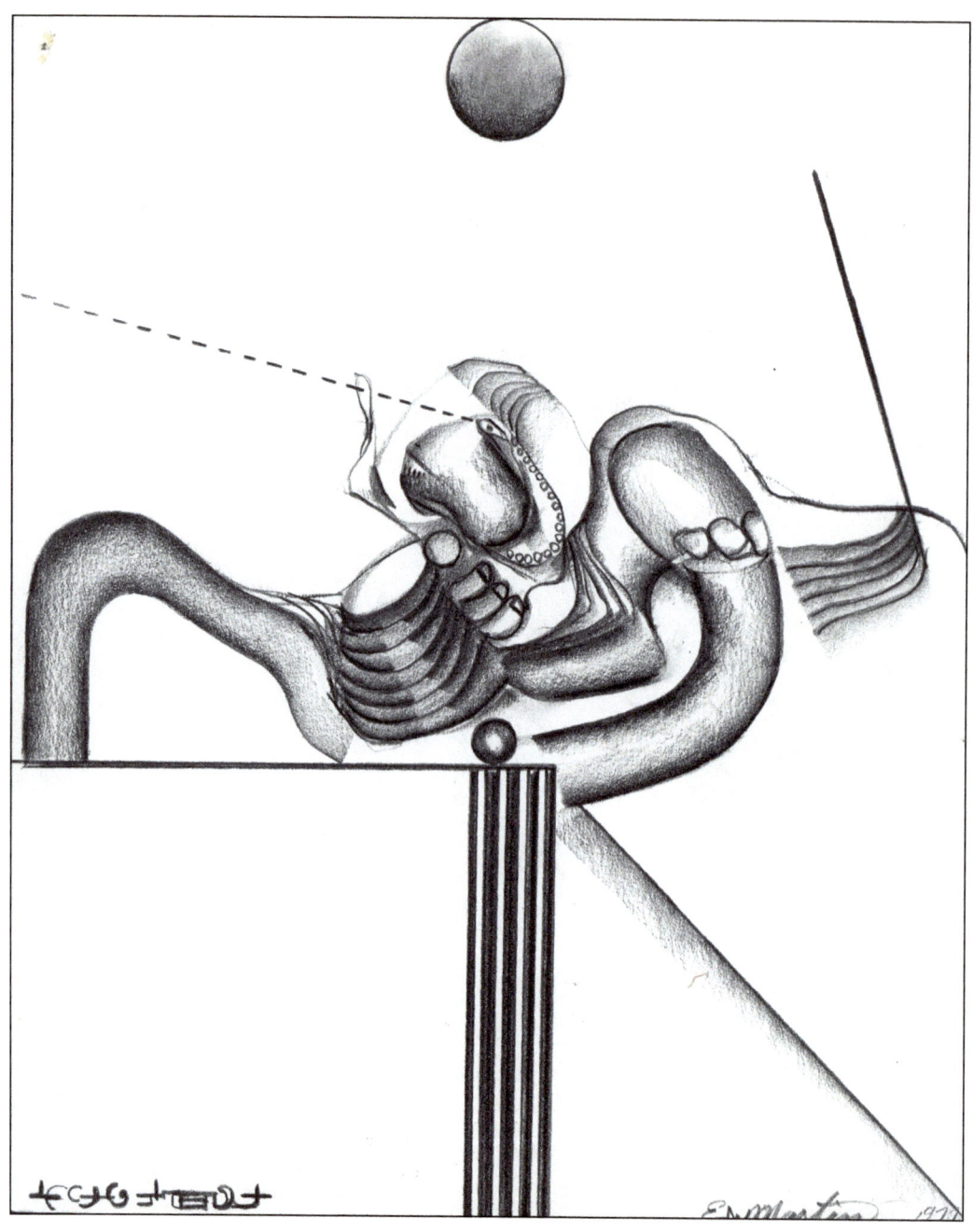

Untitled, 1977, graphite on paper, 9.5x8"

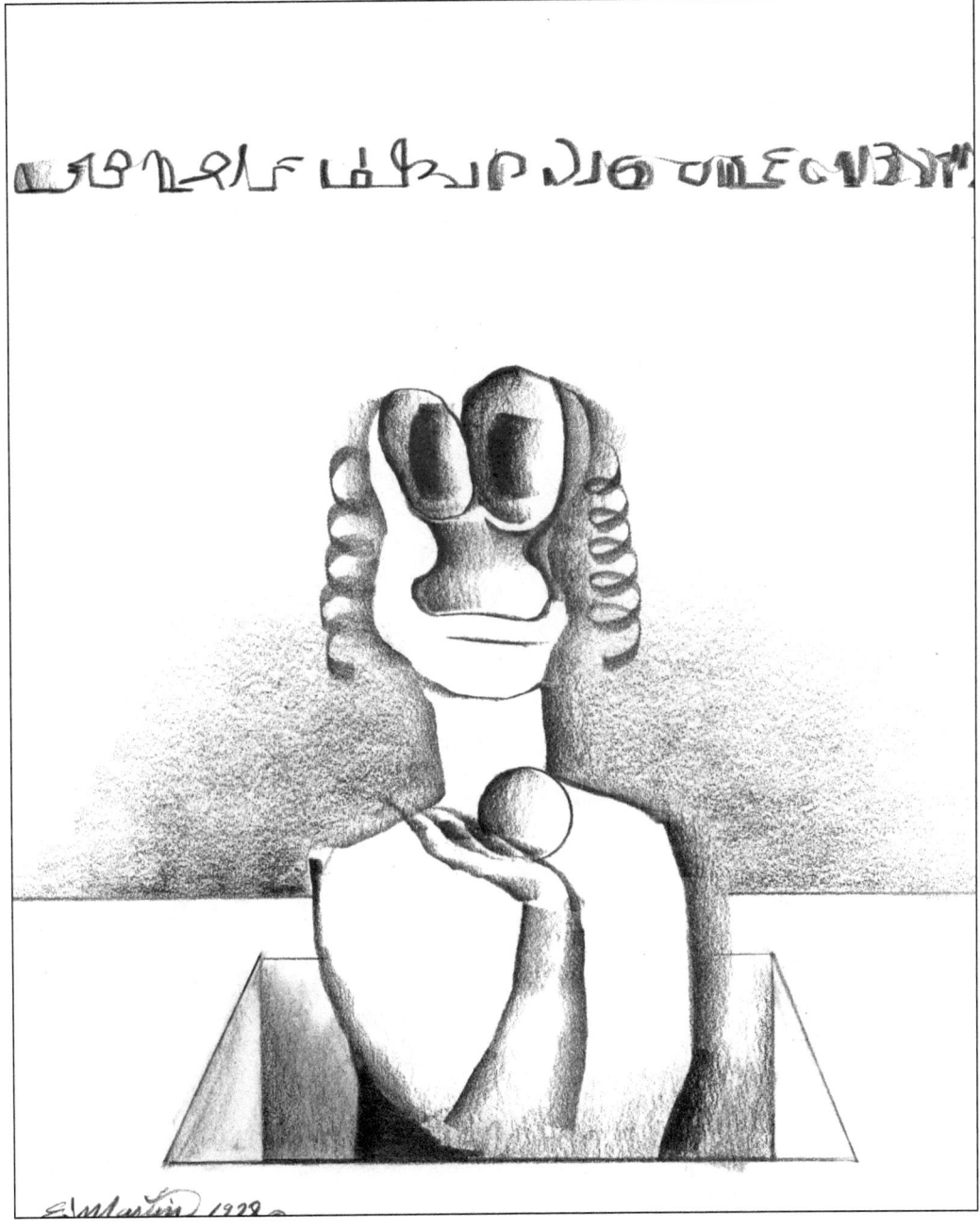

Untitled, 1978, graphite on paper, 9 3/4x8"

Eugene James Martin (b. Washington, D.C., July 24, 1938 - d. Lafayette, Louisiana, January 1, 2005) was a prolific African American visual artist.

Eugene J. Martin's art is best known for his imaginative, complex mixed media collages on paper, his often gently humorous pencil and pen and ink drawings, and his paintings on paper and canvas that may incorporate whimsical allusions to animal, machine and structural imagery among areas of "pure", constructed, biomorphic, or disciplined lyrical abstraction.

Eugene Martin's works of art can be found in numerous private art collections throughout the world, and are included in the permanent collection of the Ogden Museum of Southern Art, New Orleans; the Alexandria Museum of Art, Louisiana; the Stowitts Museum & Library in Pacific Grove, California; the Munich Museum of Modern Art; the Arthur Schomburg Center for Research in Black Culture, New York; the Mobile Museum of Art, Alabama; the Walter O. Evans Collection of African American Art in Savannah, Georgia, the Paul R. Jones Collection of African American Art at the University of Delaware, the Walter Anderson Museum of Art in Ocean Springs, Mississippi, and the Louisiana State University Museum of Art in the Shaw Center for the Arts in Baton Rouge, Louisiana.

http://www.artnet.com/awc/eugene-j-martin.html

http://www.artstor.org/what-is-artstor/w-html/col-martin.shtml

http://www.youtube.com/nemastoma